Hugo and Gayne Prellers' House of Light

By Chris Engholm with Gayne Preller Schmidt

Enjoy!

Gayne Preller Schmidt

Chris Engholm

Bentonville, Arkansas

2nd edition. Copyright, 2016. All rights reserved. For permissions, contact roadofawe@gmail.com.

An oil painting on canvas by Hugo Arthur Preller signed and dated 1893. This is likely an imagined view of an early sailing vessel ascending the Mississippi River.
Reproduction courtesy of Melanie Alumbaugh.

The Preller Collection is the earliest and largest collection of vintage photographs to emerge from the Arkansas Delta. Moreover, Gayne Laura Preller is now known to be the region's first professional female photographer.

Hugo Preller's passion for documenting the wilderness of the Delta, in tandem with Gayne's gift of putting people at ease before a lens, produced a one-of-a-kind visual history. Many are moved by the couple's fairytale bond of lifelong love and their mutual pursuit of artistic freedom. Others see within the story passion, daring, and the triumph of a woman possessed with unyielding will and social benevolence.

We hope that you will find in the Preller's life and work your own lasting impressions.

Chris Engholm, curator
Gayne Preller Schmidt, owner of
The Preller Collection

About the Photographs

The photographs and artifacts presented in this book are part of *The Preller Collection*, unless otherwise noted.

Passengers pose for a picture on the top deck of a steamboat. Photo by Hugo Arthur Preller, likely using his Pocket Autograph Kodak camera, circa 1905.

A Special Thanks To…

This book grew out of the *House of Light* exhibition, which was made possible by a grant from the Arkansas Humanities Council and the National Endowment for the Humanities. We are most grateful to the board members of the AHC for their generous support. Further, we are indebted to the Old Independence Regional Museum in Batesville, Arkansas for partnering with us in seeking funding for the exhibition.

Our Preller Advisory Group was of great assistance in the creation of both the Preller exhibit and this book; we express our gratitude to Allyn Lord, Turner Browne, Don House, Melissa Garrison, Leslie Wyman, Elyse Latella, Bill Branch, and Twyla Wright. Our academic advisors are Nancy Dowdy and Terry Gregory, and we thank them for their guidance with the *House of Light Teaching Kit*. Sabine Schmidt assisted throughout the project in the translation of Preller family letters.

Other supporting friends of the project we thank are Tommy and Jeannie Childress, Brynn Lamb, Lou Demartino, Jim Fortune, Neva Boatright, George Lankford, Kimberly Williams, Jimmy Bryant, Ambr Archard Gilbert, Mark Daniels, Erika Nelson, Patti Dell-Duchene, Elaine Partnow, Art Preller, and Laura Anne Chance. We thank Swannee Bennett, Donna Uptigrove, Carey Voss and Kim Sanders of the Historic Arkansas Museum for hosting and enhancing the exhibition.

We thank Vicki Lamar Keck, Melanie Alumbaugh, Jacksonport State Park, the Old Independence Regional Museum, the Lower White River Museum, and the University of Central Arkansas for graciously granting permission to use Preller images and objects held in their collections.

Lastly, we acknowledge photographer-historian Greer Lile for his guidance and for loaning us his model of the Preller floating gallery. We are also grateful to his sons Brett and Skip for assisting us after Greer's passing in early 2014. The *House of Light* exhibition is dedicated to the memory of Greer Lile.

Portraits of Hugo and Gayne Preller, probably made on their first floating studio in the early 1900s. Hugo is about 35 and Gayne 25 years of age.

Contents

INTRODUCTIONS	*The Preller Collection: From Discovery To Exhibition* By Chris Engholm	9
	Remembering My Grandparents By Gayne Preller Schmidt	15
Chapter 1	A Photographic Odyssey *The Preller's River Journey Begins*	17
Chapter 2	A Sojourner's Vision *Hugo Preller in God's Country*	31
Chapter 3	The First Lady of Delta Photography *Gayne Preller's Social Eye*	49
Chapter 4	The House of Doors *Painting with Light In a One-Horse Town*	67
Chapter 5	Faith In Community *The African-American Portraits*	83
Chapter 6	Preserving the Legacy *The Preller's Enduring Spirit*	103
EPILOGUE	*The Meaning of Hugo Preller's Vision*	127
SUGGESTED READING		132
INDEX		134

Preller family members on their launch in Augusta, Arkansas, circa 1910. Gayne Preller sits in the back row, third adult from the left. The Preller children sit on the gangplank in front. What appears to be an outboard engine on the john boat is actually a bait holder.

INTRODUCTIONS

The Preller Collection:
From Discovery to Exhibition

Tying up the canoe at Chickasaw Crossing -- the original name for Augusta, Arkansas – I set out to find a family descendant of the photographer Hugo Arthur Preller before paddling on. The Delta river town of Augusta is about 80 miles north of Little Rock and got its start as a cotton depot. Perched on the banks of the White River, the town had the attraction of being the highest ground on the east side of the waterway south of Batesville. Enjoying a heyday in the steamboat era, its glory faded with the coming of the railroad, and like so many Arkansas Delta towns, its decline steepened with the coming of agricultural mechanization.

Crossing a street hemmed in by listing brick facades, I caught a glimpse of a sign on a building that read, "*PRELLER TV.*" Inside the shop, I spoke to a young man who told me that the granddaughter of the Preller's still ran a dress shop on the main street through town.

That first day, I remember asking Gayne Preller Schmidt about the Preller photos. "Oh, they're here somewhere," she half-joked, rummaging in a water-stained box. When I saw that the box was filled with glassplate negatives, my heart raced and I asked her if I could digitize them for posterity. She needed no convincing that what she had shown me was historically significant, and we soon became partners in an effort to preserve "The Preller Collection."

When I finished copying the plates, Ms. Schmidt recalled that two years before she had lent a large photo album of her grandparent's photos to a friend. Luckily, we got the album back later that day because it was brimming with

"The Bounty," a watercolor by Hugo Arthur Preller painted in 1891, the earliest work of art in *The Preller Collection*.

photographs dating as early as 1895. Once we had scoured all of Ms. Schmidt's cupboards and closets, and retrieved pictures that had been lent to people over the years, we had amassed over 2,400 images, only a few of which had ever been published. When I returned to Bentonville, I restored and printed a selection of the pictures on canvas, and scholars I spoke with recognized them as significant works of historical photography. As a curator, I felt many of the images approached the level of photo art, especially the portraiture. The Preller images are little windows into a lost time, but they possess a spontaneity that makes them modern and alive for us today.

Then came the shells. Hugo Preller painted realistic river scenes on giant mussel shells he collected from Delta rivers, ten of which survive. Ms. Schmidt had also safeguarded some of Hugo Preller's oil paintings and watercolors that depict wildlife and historic places along the waterways. She told me about how her grandfather's ancestors in Germany were well-respected landscape artists, and that, "you can look them up on Wikipedia." As my enthusiasm grew, Gayne was also able to retrieve Hugo's watchmaker's desk, filled with his jeweler's tools and watchmaking parts. She had even saved the wicker chair seen in many of the portraits shot in the Preller Studio over a hundred years ago.

Scavenging in a steamer trunk, we found a cache of family documents and memorabilia. When I transcribed Hugo's letters it was like a window thrown open on the Arkansas Delta at the turn of the century. "There is no money in the country," Hugo wrote to his wife from the mouth of the White River in 1894, "but we could make a life here and live off the fat of the land." Though Hugo and Gayne Preller had passed away before I was born, as I studied the archive and listened as Ms. Schmidt shared their life story, I became deeply connected to them. The connection became a bond when we were filming actress-painter Melissa Garrison for the living history component of the exhibit, inside a replica of Mrs. Preller's original studio. Ms. Schmidt remarked that Melissa's

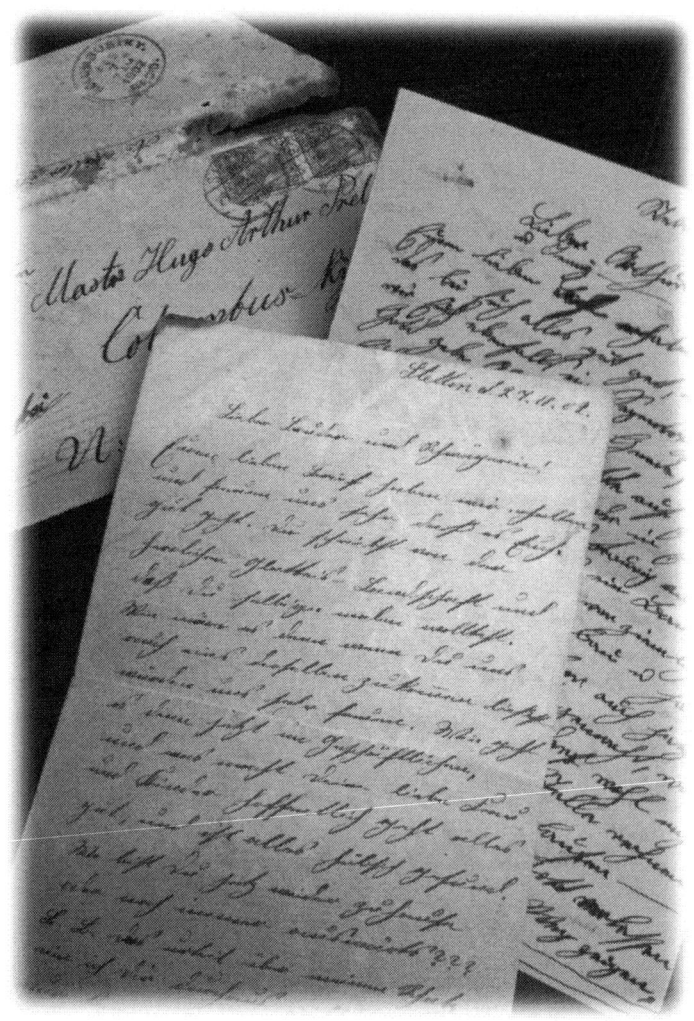

A correspondence between Hugo Preller and his mother in 1902. The language is Old German and the handwriting is an archaic style called Suetterlin script, difficult to decipher even for professional translators. The letters recently surfaced as part of the research for this book.

resemblance to her grandmother was eerie and wonderful. "It's bringing back all sorts of memories of being in the House of Doors with my grandmother." As the story crystallized, I realized that Hugo and Gayne were just as creative, persevering and adventurous as other working couples in the history of American photography. Tina Modotti and Edward Weston, Dorothea Lange and Paul Taylor—these pairings had nothing over Hugo and Gayne Preller.

Yet there were questions that needed to be answered. How was it that Hugo arrived in America as a teenager and was already a trained artisan? Were his parents related to the famous German artists, Frederick Preller the Elder and the Younger, as the Preller family believed? Did he arrive in America already practicing photography, or did he learn the craft from his young fiancé or her family? And was Hugo responsible for the Preller's archive of studio photography, or was his wife Gayne Preller in control of the studio?

Sometimes when two artists come together in union they set off in natural pursuit of an unstated notion or dream that fuels their lives and begets the unexpected. I think Hugo and Gayne experienced this, and thus, this book is an investigation of their creative powers working both individually and as a team. Who were these Delta artists and how did they create the art and photography that so evocatively recreates the place and the times in which they lived?

Amidst the old panels of the Preller's original studio, Melissa's hands lift glass negatives into the candlelight. Having climbed aboard their floating gallery, the momentum of the river takes hold. I thought of Hugo Preller's impassioned words in a 1924 letter: "Go! Write the vision, and make it plain!"

We had embarked.

Gayne Preller Schmidt, in the House of Doors studio replica at Old Independence Regional Museum in Batesville during the opening reception of the *House of Light* exhibition in April 2014.

Remembering My Grandparents

By Gayne Preller Schmidt

I write this especially for my three daughters, to tell you of things you have known and things you were not privileged to know, until now. My grandparents—your great grandparents—were two very special people, pioneers of sorts. I wish you could have known them personally, but what is contained in this book will give you the most personal relationship you could have without feeling their love and embraces as I did.

Born in the 1800s, Hugo and Gayne Preller were no less special before I met and got to know Chris Engholm; yet his insight and talent have recreated their wonderful (and difficult) lives for all of us to know, experience and appreciate. Our endeavor to weave together their art and photography with our family's history has been an amazing journey. From old photos in dusty boxes to beautiful enlargements at public exhibits, from this publication to who knows what else, we have tried to bring Hugo and Gayne to life again with words and pictures.

Girls, I want you to take time to get to know your ancestors. You would have loved them. They would have loved you. It is with great pride that I introduce you to this reclaiming of days past, which I know will help you understand from whence you came.

And blessings to you and all others who look upon these pages and experience my grandparents.

Gayne Preller Schmidt
Augusta, Arkansas

The first of two floating studio houseboats owned by the Prellers, circa 1893. Gayne Preller stands with an infant, second from the left. Those are Canada geese on the shore.

The enlarged inset shows Mrs. Preller, age 18, holding the couple's first son, Victor I, the only extant photograph of this child. *Photos courtesy of Old Independence Regional Museum.*

A Photographic Odyssey

Hugo Arthur Preller came from Germany in 1882 and spent eight years in America before meeting 16-year-old Gayne Laura Avey in Columbus, Kentucky, a small town at the confluence of the Ohio and Mississippi rivers. Her father owned the only mercantile store in town and had recently remarried. Seeing the domestic writing on the wall, Gayne began planning her escape from a future of helping in the Avey household.

Hugo and Gayne were kindred spirits; both were thirsty for adventure and saw the river as a road to freedom. They married soon after and took up residence on a houseboat. Hugo ventured to St. Louis and Memphis looking for work and acquired skills while Gayne tended to their first child. Deciding to head further south, they built a larger houseboat, replete with a photo studio, and began to float down the Mississippi River.

The Preller's floating gallery could be seen docked at different river towns for weeks at a time as Hugo repaired guns and clocks, and the couple made studio portraits of local people onboard the boat. Eventually they anchored at the mouth of Wolf River, next to the city of Memphis, and lived there for three years while their son attended school. Memphis was a rough and racially conflicted city, and soon the Prellers headed further downriver. By 1910, they had sailed up the pristine White River and settled in the port of Augusta, Arkansas, not long before known as Chickasaw Crossing. Here they put their floating studio and repair shop on dry ground.

The Preller's journey traversed six states and made contact with five major rivers. From the early 1890s to 1910, they descended the Mississippi River from St. Louis to the mouth of the White River, then ascended it to Augusta, Arkansas.

A River Journey Begins

It had taken a prodigious twist of fate to bring Hugo Preller and Gayne Avey together in the first place. Hugo was born in Berlinchen, Germany on December 30, 1865. Known as "Little Berlin," the city was annexed by Poland after World War II and lies in the northwest corner of of the country. On his naturalization papers, Hugo lists his last place of residence before emigrating to America as Stargard, Germany, now Stargard Szczecinski in Poland. Hugo's mother sent a letter to him in 1893 from Stettin, a seaport on the Baltic Sea about 25 miles from Stargard; thus, it is safe to assume that the Preller family was living in this area at the time of Hugo's departure and that he likely spent his childhood there.

Victor Preller II, the Preller's eldest son, weighs a turtle, circa 1910. He grew up in Augusta, Arkansas and opened a TV repair shop there, which remained in the Preller family until 2014.

Based on family photographs made in Germany, we know that the Preller family lived comfortably in the countryside, but the extended Preller family may have included successful artists and educators who moved in high society. For fifty years, Preller family lore had connected Hugo Arthur Preller to Friedrich Preller the Elder, and his son, Friedrich Preller the Younger, both of whom worked in Germany as professional artists in the nineteenth century. A genealogical connection has not been established as of yet, but it is possible that Hugo's father, also named Friedrich, was a cousin of Friedrich Preller the Younger. One thing is certain: when Hugo arrived in America, he was already trained in oil and watercolor painting, as well as drawing. The skills he demonstrates in his earliest works convince professional artists who have studied them that Hugo's training was likely accomplished in a professional artist's studio.

Friedrich Preller the Younger had learned in his father's studio from the age of thirteen. His father, Friedrich Preller the Elder, had left Weimar for Dresden as a young man, on the advice of Goethe. He became a student of art in Antwerp and later studied in Italy. In the 1830s, he painted scenes from Homer's *Odyssey* in Leipzig and landscapes from Oberon in Weimar. Some of his work was commissioned by the grand duchess of Weimar and preserved there, including additional scenes from the *Odyssey* painted in 1859-61. He died shortly thereafter, but his son picked up the task of painting from the epic. Preller the Younger visited Italy in search of

Friedrich Preller, from Die Gartenlaube (1864)

Given the similarity in facial features, it was tempting to conclude that Friedrich the Younger was Hugo Preller's father. On the left is a portrait of Friedrich Preller the Younger from a German publication in 1864, and on the right is a portrait of Hugo Arthur Preller's father, also Friedrich, circa 1885. The two were born about the same time in Germany.

landscapes along the Mediterranean featured in the *Odyssey*, and which he later incorporated into murals. He returned to Dresden in 1866 where he set up an art studio. In 1880, when Hugo Arthur Preller was 15 years old, he became a professor at the Dresden

Academy of Fine Arts. Hugo Preller's earliest landscape oil paintings and watercolors are similar in style to Preller the Younger's work, and his drawings appear influenced by him as well. Hugo's father was, indeed, a contemporary of Friedrich Preller the Younger. But we confirmed recently the names of their daughters and they do not match. I now believe that, via an extended family relation, young Hugo was influenced, if not trained by, Friedrich Preller the Younger (though a direct link has not been verified).

Arriving In a Promised Land

Hugo's family must have lacked the resources at the time to protect their teenage son from being drafted by setting him up to live elsewhere in Europe. His parents chose "to interrupt his schooling and hide him on a ship bound for America," says Gayne Preller Schmidt, "because they didn't want a record of his passage to become a political problem for the family in Germany." But it turned out there was a record of Hugo's passage to America among his naturalization paperwork. Based on recently discovered documents, Hugo arrived in New York City on November 17, 1882 aboard the SS Spain. The paperwork for the ship lists him as "Arthur Prelber," but other information about him was correctly transcribed. We may never know if this mistake was deliberate but it delayed confirming Hugo's birthplace and residence until 2016 when curator Carey Voss at the Historic Arkansas Museum discovered it in an online database. Hugo was seventeen years old but, alas, he was not a stowaway as the family tale had indicated. He had purchased passage in steerage on the SS Spain, the least expensive and lowest deck on the ship.

The Preller family recounts that their talented son arrived in America virtually destitute with only a Bible and some clothing. The year was 1882. Republican James Garfield was president and the United States had been unified only 17 years following the Civil War. In the South, Reconstruction had ended, tenancy and sharecropping had taken root, and the legal segregation of blacks had begun. However, the era of the New South had commenced with the tectonic shift of its cotton-based economy to one that invited northern investment in manufacturing, transportation and real estate. The era of smokestack America had arrived. Cities had sprawled and a surge of European immigrants like Hugo Preller streamed through Ellis Island.

Not long in America (and it is not known exactly how long), Hugo enlisted with the Methodist church as a circuit rider, or traveling preacher, and began proselytizing in English. On horseback, he set off to the South, into a sparsely populated wilderness following the Kentucky Trail. At the end of the Trail, he found both the Mississippi River and his future bride in Columbus, Kentucky. In Columbus at the age of 25, Hugo's life would change dramatically. Here, he worked as a sign painter and honed his skills in watch and jewelry repair and gunsmithing, exhibiting extraordinary talent and self-discipline. Yet he remained passionate about the outdoors, and also earned money fishing and trapping.

Gayne Laura Avey at age 16, not long before marrying Hugo Preller. She grew up in Columbus, Kentucky on the banks of the Mississippi River.

The Merchant's Daughter

Sixteen year-old Gayne Laura Avey had grown up in Columbus, Kentucky, situated on the eastern bank of the Mississippi River and settled in 1804. When Mark Twain passed it piloting a steamboat before the Civil War, it was known as Iron Banks, a well-defended enclave of the Chickasaw Indians. The town's "iron banks" jutted into a bend of the Mississippi and from there you could see for miles up and down the river. General Polk seized Columbus during the

A rare tintype (a photograph printed on metal) of Gayne and her sisters, probably photographed by her uncle or Hugo Preller in Columbus, circa 1895. Gayne is on the left and is likely pregnant with the couple's first child. *Photo courtesy of Vicki Keck.*

war, but ultimately the Confederate's "Gibraltar of the West" was lost to union forces and occupied.

Before the railroad came, Columbus was a distribution point for goods arriving from St. Louis, Memphis, Evansville, and Louisville; but after the railroad came, the population plummeted from 6,000 to 500 residents. By the time Gayne Avey was a toddler, Columbus was disappearing and its farmland was dying due to flooding caused by the narrowing of the river 20 miles downstream at Hickman. The installation of a river channel sealed the town's fate, as redirected river water soon tore away over half of the town.

Gayne's father, William Avey, owned a mercantile store in Columbus. He was an able entrepreneur, politically active, and his family prospered. His store was typical in that it offered everything one needed to be comfortable in the hinterland—clothes, canned food, fabric, feed, tools, tobacco. The nearby town of Cairo was a northern steamboat port too, so young Gayne was well aware of the outside world. Her father was urbane and educated; the family likely owned, or was aware of, the latest contraptions and fashions. She was a conscientious pupil, a serious piano student, and became acquainted with photography early in life. However, the Avey household was under strain. Gayne's mother had recently passed away and her father had remarried. With four siblings and a new stepmother, young Gayne found herself in an untenable situation. She wasn't fond of her new stepmother, nor the prospect of remaining at home saddled indefinitely with domestic chores. She wanted to be free, maybe get on a steamboat bound for a burgeoning city like St. Louis or Memphis. The wordly and articulate Hugo Preller strode into town at just this opportune moment.

After a brief courtship, Hugo and Gayne's wedding was held on May 24, 1892. Both were devout Christians and conservative by upbringing—hardly people one could describe as *artistes*, though it can certainly be said they were Bohemian.

A Floating Studio

A soda fountain and store photographed by Hugo Preller, circa 1900. Gayne's father owned a mercantile story in Columbus, Kentucky which probably looked similar.

Rather than build a house on a plot of land that Gayne's parents sold to the newlyweds in 1897, they built a houseboat to live in. While Gayne cared for their new baby at home, Hugo made excursions to St. Louis, about 150 miles upriver, where he peddled his talents for repairing watches and jewelry. The couple appears to have explored up and down the Big Muddy in search of opportunity and a place to eventually settle. They floated the houseboat downriver and moored it in Memphis, Tennessee around 1893 and rented a house there while Hugo marketed his services and also fished and trapped commercially. The city's rising skyline was a burgeoning symbol of the post-Reconstruction New South. But the metropolis suffered the growing problems of American urbanization and had become the most dangerous city in the South. Its Anglo-Saxon elite had enacted new laws to divide and disenfranchise African Americans; the city's earlier multiracial atmosphere had vanished in a cloud of violence and exclusion. Gayne Preller's sisters sent a series of letters to the couple during this time, pleading that they return to Columbus where life presumably would be easier. Eventually, the Prellers would return to Gayne's hometown, but not before Hugo got wind of an intriguing new business opportunity.

Gayne and three of the Preller children, circa 1900. This houseboat is smaller than the Preller's later floating studio, and has a "For Sale" sale on it. They are moored at Wolf River adjacent to the city of Memphis, Tennessee.

Opportunity Knocks In St. Louis

Though the timing is uncertain, during Hugo's working stints in St. Louis, he discovered that portrait photography was fast becoming big business. Suddenly in America everyone wanted a studio picture made, as portable cameras were not yet prevalent. Between 1885 and 1900, thousands of studios opened in American cities and towns; only the hinterland remained unserviced by a new breed of photomaking hucksters. Itinerant photographers arrived in towns that had no daguerreotype studio and set up portable studios, often in tents. In the Delta, these shooters often came by boat on the rivers, colorful characters with tales of faraway places and the latest news and

The double-deck floating studio operated by German émigré, H. O. Schroeter plied the Green River of Kentucky.

gossip. Toward the turn of the century, a number of them built floating studios on the hulls of packet boats, a small version of a steamboat, 30-to-60 feet in length. Some were sternwheel houseboats and powered by steam; others were unpowered and were towed upstream and floated downriver. Their steamboat-era charm and novelty when they moored in riverside hamlets made them irresistible to local residents and travelers alike. Sensing an opportunity, Hugo brought home samples of cabinet-card portraits made by photographers working on floating studios. When he was traversing Kentucky as a circuit rider in about 1890, Hugo happened upon a fellow German who operated a floating studio on the Green River. The Green River is 400 miles long and courses through central Kentucky before entering the Ohio River.

Traveling as a preacher, Hugo would have crossed this river on horseback when he came through the state. The man's name was H. O. Schroeter, and at this time he would have just started his business on an impressive packet boat. Schroeter's vessel featured the same lighting system as the Preller floating galleries would later, employing a skylight on the top deck. Though the Schroeter portrait that Hugo obtained is stereotypical of the studio style at the time, the similarity between it and the Preller's later work – the use of a floral backdrop, wicker sitting chair, and an ornate carpet in the foreground – at least suggests where Hugo may have learned of it firsthand. It wasn't but a couple of years before Hugo and Gayne had built their first floating studio, smaller than Schroeter's, and powered by a set of sails. The vessel was 40 feet long and a cypress hull held the deck three feet above the waterline. A steering wheel was located on the hurricane deck with internal linkage back to an extended rudder. Painted on its side in fanciful lettering were the words:

PORTRAITS. PHOTOGRAPHS.
COPYING AND ENLARGING.
ARTISTIC PAINTING.

A cabinet card found in the Preller's photo collection, likely obtained by Hugo while visiting with the photographer, H. O. Schroeter, in Kentucky.

An outdoor family portrait mounted in a cabinet card from the Preller's floating gallery, made along the Big Muddy, circa 1900.

With the launching of their first floating gallery, the Prellers had achieved the ultimate matrimony of adventure, artistic pursuit, and business prospect. What a sight the Preller houseboat would have been!

Its sails billowing, a man at the wheel on the topdeck, stove smoke spilling over the stern as Gayne cooked supper inside, and Hugo pacing the bow with eyes peeled for hidden snags. After sliding onto a sandbar, all hands hauled a cedar gangplank into place that allowed customers to come aboard to have their pictures and repairs made. Plying the river like this, the Prellers worked and raised their family on their floating studio for the next 10 years, offering their unique services to townspeople up and down the Mississippi River.

The Preller's second floating gallery, this one larger and without sails, moored to the riverbank and open for business.

Preller Timeline

1865   Hugo Arthur Preller is born in Berlinchen, in the German Empire

1875   Gayne Laura Avey is born in Columbus, Kentucky

1882   Hugo Arthur Preller arrives in New York City from

Germany, age 17

1892 Gayne Laura Avey marries Hugo Preller in Columbus, Kentucky

1894 The Prellers travel the Mississippi River in their first houseboat

1901-3 For three years, the Preller family resides in Memphis, Tennessee, returning to Columbus, Kentucky in 1904

1904 The Preller family attends the Louisiana Purchase Exposition in St. Louis

1905-10 The Prellers float the Big Muddy to the White River, and then ascend it to Augusta, Arkansas. They settle there and open the Preller Variety Shop

1914-21 Hugo Preller paints *Summertime in Augusta*, as well numerous scenes and events on large mussel shells

1910-52 Gayne Preller operates a portrait studio in Augusta, photographing residents as well as farmers living outside town

1950 Hugo Arthur Preller passes away at age 85

1952 Gayne Preller closes the Preller photography studio; she passes away 3 years later

"I sought all my life a proper understanding of things mysterious and invisible."

Hugo Arthur Preller, 1924

A Sojourner's Vision

Hugo Preller arrived in the New World driven by a vision of divine power that he had experienced firsthand. As a young boy in Germany, one freezing morning he ambled in the snow along the shore of a lake near his village. In the grey silence, he heard a hissing noise beneath the ice. A fissure opened and a ball of fire suddenly rose, then widened into a conflagration of flames in midair. The boy gazed in amazement as the billowing flames gathered and then flew past him and toward the horizon. The vision would haunt Hugo the rest of his life, and impel him on a quest for answers about the nature of God's will and eternal salvation.

Twenty years later, in the far reaches of the Mississippi Delta, Hugo discovered an untamed paradise, where a person "could live off the fat of the land." He ventured up and down the rivers in search of paying prospects to support his new family. Soon he found his skills were marketable, and he assisted his young wife Gayne in manifesting her dreams as well. Recognizing that the virgin wild of the Delta was fast-changing, Hugo recorded its transformation. He made outdoor pictures and painted realistic river scenes, some on enormous mussel shells, that are of great historical value today.

Each chapter of this book begins with a summary from the original display panels for each section of the *House of Light* exhibition.

An oil painting by Hugo Preller created in 1904 depicting his mother, father, and younger sister in Germany. The painting is based on a photo postcard that he received from the family.

Hugo Preller in God's Country

From the time he left Germany, it would be seven years until Hugo would marry Gayne Laura Avey in a tiny flood-prone town at the terminus of the Kentucky Trail. These years remain an undocumented chapter of his adventurous life. From his later letters and writings, it is only known with certainty that he possessed a tenacious intellect and some previous training in jewelry repair and landscape painting. (Perhaps his father had worked in these professions.) And that he was deeply religious. In a letter years later, he recounts being "inclined to be of religious tendencies from [his] earliest days of childhood." He mentions his mother teaching him Bible philosophy and an early "ardent desire to enter the ministry," and "become a Pastor and Shepherd of the Fold of Christ." His letters also confirm that once in America, he soon became "a licensed preacher and active member in the [Methodist] church."

In its expansion efforts at the time, the Methodist Church was quite accommodating toward intrepid preachers, even if they lacked refinement and extensive religious training. Preaching in the wild was only for the rough and ready. One early Methodist preacher described the difficulties of circuit riding in the region: "The Mississippi was not levied then...and preachers...went to their appointments in skiffs and canoes, crossed the bayous on the backs of their horses, or if that was too hazardous they got a few logs together, tied them with grapevines....[These preachers] were the 'swamp angels' of that day."

Evidenced by his writings less than a decade later, Hugo was a quick study and had mastered English; his tattered and heavily inscribed Bible survives as testimony to his erudition. Carrying this book as he rode, he proselytized at camp meetings and on dusty street corners in burgeoning hamlets along the Trail, and reported success in engaging listeners and expanding the flock. He ultimately became a member of the Church's "South" Conference, which was headquartered in Memphis.

A Frontier Trek

Hugo's exact route to Columbus, Kentucky can only be guessed. It's likely that he followed all or part of the Wilderness Trail made renown by Daniel Boone and other fabled frontiersmen, as it was the only known route from New York and Boston to the New Territories, crossing the Cumberland Gap and arriving not far from Columbus, Kentucky and the Mississippi River. The American wilderness enchanted Hugo as it had another peripatetic visitor from Germany, the writer and sportsman Friedrich Gerstaeker, forty years before.

After arriving in Columbus at the age of 25, Hugo's life would change dramatically. It wasn't long before he had refined his skills in both jewelry and watch repair and was marketing these services with a calling card. Being in Columbus put Hugo within striking distance of two burgeoning river metropolises—St. Louis and Memphis. (The address on his card was in St. Louis, indicating he may have set up a shop there.) Hugo could hop on a steamboat and make his way for St. Louis, Natchez, and Memphis without more hassle than purchasing a steamboat passage.

But the call of the wild bedeviled him. Although

A huge mussel shell painted with a realistic view of Forest Park in St. Louis by Hugo Preller. The painting is dated 1918, indicating that Hugo continued to visit and perhaps work in the city even after the family settled in Augusta.

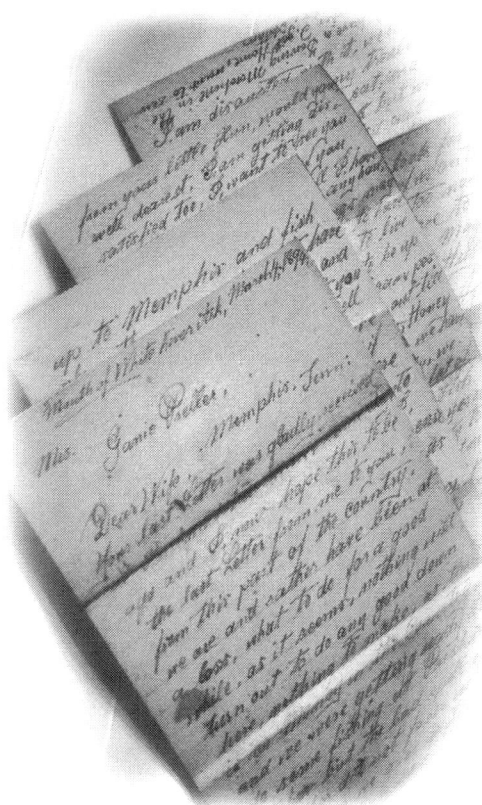

Hugo Preller's letter from the mouth of the White River to his wife, written in 1894 when he was 29. He informs her that although there is "no money in the country," the family could live off the land in the river bottoms and escape the troubles of city life. Notice he spells his wife's name, "Ganie." She later decided she liked "Gayne" better, so that spelling has been in this book.

it had been a half-century since Mark Twain published his book, *Life On the Mississippi,* Hugo would have heard both steamboat and mountain-man lore, and I think their romance took deep root in him. Around the time they were married, Gayne Preller made the earliest photograph of her husband in *The Preller Collection*, when he was in his late twenties. (See photo on page 30.) Here, at least in image, Hugo measures up to the Kentucky frontiersmen he admired. Gayne made a number of prints from this glass negative and attempted to hand-color them, adding daubs of red to embellish the wound on the fawn and the texture of the rock. (The rocky terrain is probably in the hills surrounding Columbus.) Judging from the work she dedicated to the picture, she must have appreciated her new husband's frontiersman persona, and was also likely impressed by the utilitarian aspect of the hunter as well, who was putting food on her family's table.

Always yearning to escape the urban bustle and connect with bountiful nature, Hugo soon struck out south and into open country. In 1894, in a small riverboat with a fishing partner, he left his wife and child in Memphis and drifted downriver to the confluence of the Arkansas River. About 200 miles south, lush and uninhabited wilds stirred his imagination and animated a dream for his family's future. He found there the swift and sinuous White River, which penetrated 700 miles into the fertile womb of the Arkansas Delta, then an unimaginably vast forest of hardwood and wildlife-teeming swampland. The further he explored the primeval river bottoms, the more he came to eschew the frantic lifestyle of the city. Gerstaeker, whose adventure novels and accounts the Prellers might have read in Germany, had been bewitched by this region too, and wrote about the White River in glowing terms. It flowed clearer than any tributary the Prellers had floated and the trappers and traders there found a rich supply of game. Small towns were sputtering to life after the ravages of the Civil War 30 years before, and everyone had a gun to repair.

    Here, in a riverboat drifting beneath mammoth cypress trees top-heavy with roosting egret and geese, Hugo wrote to his young wife waiting for him back in Memphis.

A cypress swamp near the mouth of the White River in 2013, like Hugo would have seen during his hunting and fishing journeys in this region.
Photo: Chris Engholm.

Hugo's Letter from the White River
(Edited for readability)

From the mouth of White River of Arkansas, March 4, 1894.

Mrs. Gayne Preller, *Memphis, Tenn:*

Dear Wife,

Some days ago, I gladly received your last letter at Poshmatahaw, Miss. I now hope this to be my last letter from this part of the country. For a good while, we have been at a loss as to what to do. It seems nothing will turn out any good down here, nothing to earn, as there is no money in the country. We were getting ready to do some fishing at Poshmatahaw but a bad spell of weather did not favor us, so we gave up the idea and plan to come back to Memphis and fish there. We need more nets to do any good and I'm not satisfied without you being here, no how.

I could be well contented down here and we could do tolerable well too. But I don't want to go to the expense of bringing you down now, as I am surely going to St. Louis by the first of July 1894, if I live and keep well. Well Gayne, you poor little thing, I am happy to hear you would rather be in a flat boat than be away from your little Hun. I am

Hugo the outdoorsman, with one of his sons and a string of squirrels, probably photographed by Gayne Preller, circa 1900 when he was age 35.

getting dissatisfied too. I want to see you and the baby and kiss all of you again soon. For that is all I have to enjoy in this life, and no matter how things may be hereafter, I am going to have you with me even if we have to live like Gypsies. If I can possibly do so, I expect to be up on the next boat. Honey, this letter leaves me well and doing fine physically. We have been living off the fat of the land, and have game or fish of some kind every day. Yes, all of us would have plenty to eat and to live off down here, but money is none in this country and that is all a person can get along with in a city. I am disgusted with it. We could live here, without any trouble and have plenty to eat, and a little money besides, but we are all tore up and unsettled right now. Things have to take a turn in the near future, so you may look for me on the next boat, and to stay too. With regards and love to you and the Baby.

    I am your loving husband.

Hugo Arthur Preller

A Revealing Correspondence

This letter speaks to us intimately from 120 years ago. Hugo is 29 and Gayne is 19. The couple has been writing to each other regularly in the spring of 1894, two years after they were married. Hugo had been away for some months, and it is clear that he was away often seeking opportunities for the family to earn a living. The letter is addressed to Gayne in Memphis, where the family has resided for two or three years. Gayne is there caring for the couple's infant son, Victor.

    Hugo has his eyes open for a new place for the family to live. He has received a letter from Gayne while in "Poshmatahaw" (now Muscle Shoals), and he has fished near Arkansas City, on the rivers that converge nearby. He refers to his whereabouts as "the Mouth of White River" and mentions that this part of the country is rich in game and fish. A trapping partner accompanies Hugo in a small riverboat. The two had intended on fishing but the weather has stymied their plans, so they plan to return north to Memphis to fish

A new year's card created by the Prellers, circa 1910. The image is actually a photograph of a painting by Hugo Preller that depicts a steamboat and other vessels passing the town of Crocketts Bluff on the White River.

because they need more nets "to do any good." Thus it is assumed they are acting as commercial fishermen attempting to produce salable numbers of buffalo fish and catfish, and earn money doing so.

However, it becomes clear that Hugo has been down-and-out for some time and admits that this sparsely populated region offers little opportunity. He is discouraged, writing, "Nothing will turn out any good down here, as there is no money in the country." He does not mention preaching, painting, nor photographing the scenery and thus, does not seem to have artistic ambitions as of yet. We learn, however, that he works intermittently in St. Louis, where he plans to return four months hence to work, presumably

An enormous hoop net for catching catfish and buffalo fish. Hugo mentions such nets in his 1894 letter from the White River, and a number of them appear stacked atop the Preller's floating studio in some photographs.

repairing watches and jewelry.

Hugo speaks contemptuously about city life and wants to live closer to the land. He evidently loves the country and wants to escape the city but thus far, he can't conceive of how to support his family in the wilderness. With all his complaints, however, he reports that he would be content moving to this part of the country, and that together they could do "tolerably well" there. The letter "leaves" the two trappers well; he mentions that they are healthy, a hint that this far south the prevalence of malarial disease was high. They are finding game and fish plentiful and are eating well, which suggests to him that, "Yes, all of us would have plenty to...live off." He does not mention, however, what services they might sell in this region.

Hugo's vision for the couple's future was clearly forming. He misses his wife and baby, stating, "for that is all that I have got...to enjoy in this life." He teases Gayne for wanting to be with her "little Hun," even if it means traveling in a damp riverboat. He wants Gayne to be near him "even if they have to live like Gypsies." This statement can certainly be called foreshadowing.

Hugo's self-convincing continues. He is "disgusted" with the fact that to live in a city requires money. "[Money] is all a person can get along with in a city," he complains, referring to Memphis

The Preller's second floating studio, circa 1905. The photograph is inscribed on the rear in Gayne Preller's hand: "Came from St. Louis on this boat. Had been in storm in St. Louis." She also notes the place as Wolf River and the kids (left to right) as Dewey, Max, and Victor II.

and St. Louis. Again he proclaims to Gayne that the river mouth beckons: "We could live here, without any trouble." But there are obstacles, as we learn when he states, ominously: "But we are all tore up and unsettled." It's not clear what exactly this means. Perhaps they haven't been able to find work in Memphis. Perhaps they have strained relations with the Avey family back in Columbus. Certainly they are disillusioned and things haven't gone as planned. Nor would they in the near future, as tragedy struck the newlyweds shortly after this letter was written.

When Victor was just two years old, in 1895, he crawled out of his crib in the stern of the houseboat and fell into the river. The couple had each thought the unattended child was being watched by the other. They retrieved the body from under the gang plank of the boat in just a few feet of water. The Prellers placed a funeral notice in the newspaper announcing a memorial, with the words regarding their first child: "He left a world of vanity, of trouble and deceit, to live with Jesus evermore, where some day we shall meet." The couple is said to have spoken rarely about the incident in ensuing years, and it is not known where the child is buried.

The Prellers Return Home

For the next several years, the Prellers lived on their houseboat back up north in Columbus, near Gayne's family. They restarted their lives and, in 1896, Gayne gave birth to a second boy, whom the couple named Victor II. Hugo built up his jewelry repair business in St. Louis and the couple honed their photography skills, producing some of their most elegant portraits aboard their floating studio. Hugo also painted the first of his collection of studio backdrops at this time. In 1904, now with two young boys (Victor II and Dewey), the family attended the Columbian Exposition in St. Louis. This vacation must have been exhilarating, especially for Gayne, since new developments in photographic technology were featured at the show. Also, during this period, they purchased their second floating studio, which was larger than the first. On its side, Hugo painted the words---

PRELLER'S PHOTO
AND REPAIR SHOP

It appears that duties were becoming divided, with Hugo taking responsibility for repairs and Gayne focusing on the photo studio, though we cannot be sure exactly when this transition occurred.

A Spiritual Ecologist

Though little more is known about the Preller's years prior to their arriving in Augusta, one senses in Hugo's writings an unrelenting urge to return to the White River and escape the big city once and for all. As he traversed the American wilderness peddling his talents—fishing, hunting, and seeking spiritual solace—he became nothing less than an environmental documentarian, a visual historian of the region's changing ecology. Mr. Preller was a natural documentary artist, with his enthusiasm for the real and his proclivity to record without bias or heavy interpretation. He was enthralled by the changes along the river and became an itinerant recorder on film, canvas, and on the inside of huge mussel

"Summertime In Augusta," painted by Hugo Preller in 1914, shows a barge of logs being delivered to the mill at Augusta, and the Preller family launch bringing family members across the White River to a swimming beach. (This launch appears in the photograph on page 8.)

shells. Floods, fires, steamboats, highway construction, clearing the forest, a button factory, the opening of a new rail station—these were radical changes and he recorded them dutifully. Photographs of this sort would have had little commercial value then, but for us, Hugo's outdoor catalog illustrates a tale about the building of the New South in the Delta region.

In the natural surroundings of the Delta, Hugo would find a muse, as well as a profound spiritual connection. He expressed this relationship like his ancestors in Germany had, in paintings of landscapes and wildlife. As of 1891, and perhaps before, he painted scenes from life of places he visited along the rivers. His earliest artwork that survives is a still-life watercolor of a string of slain birds (see page 10), a fine illustration by any standard that demonstrates his acute powers in observing the natural world. In 1893, he painted a large sailing vessel moving up the Mississippi River (see page 2), an image as evocative as a passage from Twain's *Adventures of Huckleberry Finn*. In the 1910s, he would begin a series of paintings on shells, including views of Des Arc, Crocketts Bluff, and Forest Park in St. Louis. His depiction of the button factory at DeValls Bluff hangs today in the Lower White River Museum in Des Arc and the rest are in the custody of Preller family members. His most ambitious surviving work is "Summertime in Augusta," (at left), painted in 1914, a 36-inch wide panorama that accurately depicts the riverbank and timber mill that operated in Augusta at that time.

 The cumulative sum of Hugo's surviving artwork is decisive testimony of a laudable talent, and evidence that, if he had been financially able to focus on art making alone, he could have achieved notoriety among southern artists of his time.

A Wilderness Conscience. Artistically and spiritually in sync with his surroundings, and deeply troubled by the destruction of the southern wilderness, Hugo cultivated an ecological ethic that was 50 years ahead of its time. He wrote (in English) prophetically in 1924:

> *No one can fail to take notice of...the problem of Man, his origin and final destiny; and the possible conditions confronting coming generations in view of the inevitable depletion of resources, as compared to growing demands on account of increase in world population....Those things are indeed of most absorbing...concern in the minds of the wise of this world.*

"From Arkansas, Around the World," circa 1900.
Proof that the Delta was a magnet for colorful characters, this itinerant odd jobber totes his tool-sharpening apparatus from farmstead to shop in a homemade cart. We wonder how far he made it.
Photo by Hugo Preller.

A Haunting Vision

Hugo Preller represents a true spiritual seeker whose journey began with a vision he experienced as a child, summarized at the start of this chapter. Given the formative role it played in Hugo's childhood and adult personality, I include below an account of the experience in his own words, from a letter written to a Methodist church official in 1924:

> *One winter's evening when but a mere child, while alone out in the open, while carefree and skipping in the snow along the shore of a lake -- with all nature at rest and hardly a sound anywhere -- there suddenly arose, perhaps thirty feet from the shore, out of water and through ice and snow, a bright flickering. As I beheld this strange vision, the fire rapidly contracted until, in midair above the lake, hung a ball of fire motionless. It stayed there only for a moment and then suddenly became animated and moved toward me, gaining in speed at every foot of distance so that by the time it was passing only a few inches in front of my eyes, it was making a rushing, hissing sound like a ball fired from a cannon -- which proved its density. As my eyes followed its flight, it passed through a board fence and across a vacant lot at the outskirts of the village, and disappeared in the distance. What was it?*

What was it, indeed! After this experience, Hugo was forever sensitive to the supernatural in his midst, and for the rest of his life he would seek an "understanding of things mysterious and invisible." The unseen powers he witnessed made him feel chosen and spurred him in pursuit of ultimate truths about eternal life and salvation, concepts he studied in the Bible as a child under the tutelage of his devout mother. Later in life, he came to believe that this experience ordained him for special work on behalf of God, and compared his vision to that of Moses when he was called to deliver Israel out of bondage.

>And Moses went up to the mount,
>And the sight of the glory of the Lord was like devouring fire....

> And Moses got onto the mount and went into the midst of the cloud.
>
> *From* Exodus 25:15-18

His grail-like search for an understanding of his vision's meaning, and what it might portend, would last for decades. Not until his final days would it finally reveal its secrets.

Hugo Arthur Preller with his four sons – Victor, Dewey, Hugh, and Max – in the 1920s outside the Preller Variety Store in Augusta, Arkansas.

Gayne Laura Preller, photographed by her husband in the Preller floating studio, circa 1900, when she was 25 years of age.

The First Lady of Delta Photography

Delta historians always assumed Hugo Preller was responsible for the lion's share of Preller photographs. It is now known that Gayne Preller produced virtually all of the Preller portraiture after the family arrived in Augusta, circa 1910. Of the 2,400 pictures in *The Preller Collection*, an estimated 1,900 were made by Gayne. This is not to lessen the value of Hugo's contribution, but to emphasize that Gayne Preller is perhaps the earliest—and certainly the most prolific—female photographer in the Arkansas Delta.

Like nearby Heber Springs portraitist Mike (Meyer) Disfarmer, Gayne did not considered herself an "artist," nor did she seek inspiration from, or collaborate with, other professional photographers. Simply put, studio portraiture for her was a livelihood. It kept the wolves from the door. Indeed, during the Depression, Gayne's income helped the Prellers survive, and she continued to earn a living operating the business after Hugo Preller passed away.

However, like her husband, Gayne Preller was an artist in the classic sense. Her portraits are energetic and fresh over 100 years since their making. She individualizes her sitters, seeking constantly to reveal their innermost character. She's not a social reformer like Dorothea Lange, or a cultural interpreter like Jacob Riis. She's not interested in pictorialist themes as was Julia Margaret Cameron, or even light, shadow and form as was Alfred Stieglitz. But she was keen and sensitive in eliciting human idiosyncrasies. She bequeaths to us a gallery full of living, breathing Delta personalities.

Christmas on the Preller's floating studio, circa 1904. The boat was likely moored near Columbus, Kentucky at the time, where Victor II (left) was attending school. On the table sits a stereoscope (a three-dimensional photo viewer), perhaps a gift from one of the Preller spouses to the other.

Gayne Preller's Social Eye

The spark for creating the *House of Light* exhibition occured during an interview for a spoken history of the Ozarks' White River.[1] I had approached Gayne Preller Schmidt with the idea of including the Preller family story in the book. As we hunched over catfish sandwiches at a diner in Augusta, I asked if her grandmother had accompanied Hugo on his hunting journeys in the river bottoms. Like other history buffs in the region, I believed at the time that all Preller photos had been created by Hugo Preller, with Gayne playing the role of the dutiful wife who developed some of his dry plates. Our conversation went like this—

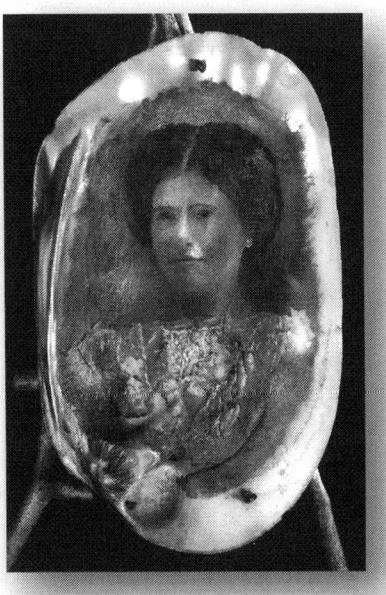

This elegant portrait of Gayne Preller circa 1915 is signed but not dated. Its condition is extremely poor and has been digitally restored here.

> Chris: "If Hugo went on a trip down the river, would Gayne go with him?"
> Ms Schmidt: "No. He was fishing and trapping animals and selling fur."
> Chris: "And Gayne would stay in Augusta and take care of the home?"
> Ms. Schmidt: "She did all of the photography in the studio there."
> Chris: "So Hugo was not involved with the studio photography in the House of Doors?"
> Ms. Schmidt: "No, he took the outside pictures and she did the inside pictures."
> Chris: "So really, they were equal partners in the photography

---

[1] The book is *White River Memoirs: the Spoken History of a Liquid Legend*, and includes an interview with Gayne Preller Schmidt.

> business?"
> Ms. Schmidt: "Yes, but he was the peddler."

For me, this conversation was a revelation. Gayne Preller had not just processed Hugo's glass negatives and films, but had singlehandedly operated the Preller studio in Augusta. Hugo was only responsible for the landscape and group portrait photography. In fact, I later discovered that Gayne's interest in photography began as a teenager and that perhaps she had introduced Hugo to the art form.

This is the earliest surviving photograph made by Gayne Preller. It is probably a view of Columbus, Kentucky, though this is difficult to confirm since half of the town was taken by the Mississippi River in ensuing years. The inherent mystery of the composition, the print quality, and mounting all belie the fact that it was made by a teenager.

An Early Introduction to Photography

One winter's day, newly-married Gayne Preller set up a view

camera in her hometown along an avenue and made a gorgeous image of horse-drawn carriages in the snow (at left). It is the earliest surviving picture that can be verified to have been created by her, because it is marked with her personal photographer's stamp. The year was 1895 and she was 19 years old. Already, Gayne considered herself a commercial photographer.

Before it became clear about Gayne Preller's actual role in the Preller studio, no one asked who introduced her to photography. Even as I came to understand her true role in the Preller studio, I

Obscured by the damaged area, a man sits holding a brush. He is most likely I. C. Avey, whose service is listed on the right end of the cannon. On the left end is the name of a "Photographer." At enlargement, his last name also appears to be Avey, probably an uncle of Gayne Preller.

continued to assume her artistic and technically minded husband had introduced her to photography. How had Gayne learned photography at so young an age, and how had she become so professionally serious about it? Did Hugo arrive when he was 25, as a circuit rider with portable camera in hand, and teach his 16-year-old fiancé the art of picture taking? Although Hugo was a gifted visual artist, I could not fathom how he would have known

A portrait typical of the formal poses seen in the earliest Preller work on board their first floating gallery, circa 1900. Light from above has entered through a skylight in the roof of the boat, and appears to have been bounced onto the face with a reflector. The camera work and attention to styling are exemplary.

photography before arriving in Kentucky on horseback. I then realized there were no existing photographs in the Preller archive from Hugo's journey down the Kentucky Trail, while there were photographs from Columbus that were made before Hugo and Gayne were married. The half-destroyed photo from the archive (above) provides an explanation. The old cannon barrel has just been painted. A can of paint brushes sits on the right end of the barrel above the name, "I. C. Avey," who was Issac Avey, a brother of Gayne's father. He was a sign painter and, given the hand holding the paintbrush, the obscured sitter on the left is likely him. It is not known who the boy might be.

Then I realized that the left side of the cannon features the word "Photographer." At magnification, I found that the name of the photographer is J. [?]. Avey, and thus, is likely another brother of Gayne's father whom we have not identified yet. He likely made the picture, around 1890. Hence, we now know that professional photography was already being practiced in Gayne's family when she grew up in Kentucky, before Hugo's arrival. This explains why her first pictures are imprinted with her stamp. She was already a serious photographer when her husband-to-be trotted into town.

Aboard the Floating Gallery

Not long after they were married, the Prellers built a simple houseboat in which they would start their family. We have few pictures from this time during Gayne's formative career, probably because she was a teenager raising children and did not produce much portraiture. By 1898, however, the couple had built their first of two floating studios and opened for business on the Mississippi River offering portraits, copying and repairs of watches and jewelry. Unfortunately, there is no extant logbook of the voyage or diary that recounts the places and people they encountered, or the hardships they endured, while living on the river. And no images survive that depict the interior of the floating studio.

The portraits that the Prellers made on the boat were formal, for which they used modified (reflected) light and elaborate staging. Some of these portraits are enlarged and many are elaborately mounted in cabinet cards. The enlarging of photographs was a new offering at this time, and it's a mark of the Prellers business acumen that they made it central to their business model.

Throughout this period, it is unclear how the couple divided photographic duties. For certain, Gayne processed glass plates and made prints, and she likely worked with Hugo creating photographs and engaging customers as well. Hugo was responsible for a painted set of studio backdrops, three of which portray scenes along the banks of the Mississippi; they would be priceless if they had survived. Since a highly stylized approach delineates this period of Preller photography from Gayne's independent studio work after 1910, my feeling is that Hugo and Gayne produced these early pictures working together.

Settling In the Arkansas Delta

It was not until the family settled on dry land in 1910, and the children were older, that Gayne hit her stride as a portrait photographer. In Augusta (population approximately 3,000 at the time), she soon became a fixture in the community. Her photography grew less formal and less exquisitely lighted than what the couple produced on the floating studio, and she made few enlargements, focusing instead on delivering postcard contact prints at a reasonable price. The work is spontaneous and sensitive to the personality of the person being depicted. While Hugo continued to photograph -- and paint -- outdoor scenes, Gayne was said to rarely leave the confines of her studio shop, where I estimate she produced 3,000 portraits of people in Woodruff County, Arkansas, between 1908 and 1952.

Gayne Preller's business card. She used only her initials to hide the fact that her business was female-owned, says her granddaughter, Gayne Preller Schmidt. The service of "Kodak developing" meant that she would accept undeveloped films from clients and handle sending it to Kodak for processing and enlarging.

The Preller Partnership

Throughout Gayne's career, however, her husband remained an essential catalyst for her success. It was he who likely conceived the floating gallery idea in the first place and possessed the know-how to build the boat. Later in Augusta, Gayne Preller Schmidt recalls that it was Hugo's popularity and skills that kickstarted Gayne's portrait business, which grew quickly, in part, because Hugo repaired guns for the men of the area. "Once they came into his shop," says Ms. Schmidt, "they learned of Gayne's adjacent studio and brought their wives along the next time." Hence, Hugo's work helped to place Gayne center stage to greet a parade of archetypical characters to be photographed, from suffragettes, catfishers and farm bureau agents, to drummers, river rats and sharecroppers. As Augusta's only established community photographer, she would record the visual history of a Delta community as written on the elegiac faces that Hugo helped bring through the Preller doors.

And Gayne would continue to use Hugo as a male front for the store, and had "G. L. Preller" printed on her calling card, instead of her full name, to appear as a male-run business. As the years passed, however, Hugo grew shy with people and left customer relations to Gayne. As an older man, he became more and more introverted and rarely shared his feelings in conversation, even with his grandchildren.

Gayne Preller photographs her sons Victor II and Dewey on a river bank, likely near Columbus, Kentucky, around 1904 when Gayne was 29, the same year the family attended the St. Louis Exposition. Gayne has released the shutter using an air bulb in her right hand, and is withdrawing the film back with her left. The family might have come to this setting by way of the sailboat visible at the far left.

Meanwhile, growing more confident in her work, Gayne's personality evolved in the opposite direction. As she got older, she became increasingly engaged with the unique residents of her community.

The Evolution of a Portraitist

Making pictures for over 60 years, Gayne Preller was a crossover portraitist, straddling the eras of traditional and modern photography. She started professional photography as a rather shaky pictorialist. The typical pictorialist aimed for poetic, melodramatic effects produced by the use of soft focus and elaborate set staging, reminiscent of the earliest Hollywood movies. Storyline was emphasized, often excessively rendered as if the camera could "capture," in an instant, what a painter captured after weeks of effort on a canvas. Gayne didn't photograph soft-focused nymphs dipping palms into moonlit rivulets, but she did strive for painterly and romantic effects in her earliest work. She never set up staged scenes from The Passion or the Rubáiyát, yet -- especially with her early hand-tinted work -- she energetically pursued pictorial objectives and never turned away from the sentimental traditions of the style. And,

"The Outing," by Gayne Preller, circa 1904. This portrait of a group is a black and white print that Gayne has hand painted. She has etched in crude water reflections and tinted the shrubbery green. The posing and composition, however, are superb.

unknowingly, she continued to defend pictorial practices with her long exposures in natural light and soft focus due to shallow depth of field.

The image above is of a women's outing at the river. This is a posed environmental portrait made about 1900 when Gayne was in her early twenties. She has painted the photograph, giving the banks a green hue and emphasis to the reflections in the water. Like other surviving examples of her photo tinting, the work here is fairly amateur. Though she sought the painterly, the vision was elusive to her untrained hand. Why Hugo did not assist her in this tedious endeavor is not known. Though Gayne proved not to be an exemplary pictorialist in her early work, she was, indeed, a natural portraitist. Making family pictures was Gayne's forte, and

"Hats On, Hats Off," circa 1910. Fashionable ladies of Augusta induced to doff their feathered hats.

to have overpowered it with forced pictorial technique would have obscured the thing we enjoy most about her oeuvre—its straightforwardness.

Every Picture Tells a Story. Photographers of Gayne's generation learned that portrait making was a spontaneous art, an improvisation that revealed, however unintended, the relationship between subject and photographer. Gifted at facilitating spontaneous humor and expression in a portrait, Gayne could put people at ease immediately, and many of her subjects responded. She understood that in play was revelation of character. A portrait studio is a stage set for the minor performance of spontaneous expression, and Gayne could generate extempore behavior and antics on demand. You can almost hear her insistent voice with the three overdressed matrons on the previous page—"Ladies, now we're going to try something wild—off with your hats!"

She relished capturing people being more than their day-to-day selves. She got her sitters to express something long hidden. I think she developed this talent by constantly making pictures of Preller family members in her studio. The family snapshot was still a novelty and Gayne's was the first generation to use a camera to record family passages—births, events, even deaths. Indeed, as few other residents of the Delta did at the time, she memorialized the life of her family using photography. In the same way, she captured her neighbors as well.

The backside of this peculiar print reads, "Red Cross Society." It was made on the floating gallery using a backdrop and straw in the foreground. One can only imagine the festive occasion that instigated this humorous picture, circa 1905.

Physiognomy of a Community

Walker Evans' WPA photographs were said by one writer, "to put the physiognomy of the nation on your table." Gayne shot during the same tumultuous period of history, but what she recorded is the physiognomy of a community. As one of the earliest female photographers in the Delta to peer through a lens, she photographed a single community over a vast span of time. In her work, every class and type of person makes at least a cameo appearance. Yet she never displays a WPA-like interest in making images that promote social reform. She created a visual history of a community of personalities, and this is how her work should be enjoyed today.

Striving for a perfectly exposed print, Gayne made six attempts of this portrait, circa 1900. Each is a separate contact print on photo postcard paper.

Gayne Preller was part of a national emergence of women photographers -- including Dorothea Lange, Laura Gilpin, Imogen Cunningham, and Gertrude Käsebier -- but she was not typical for many reasons. First, she was rural in character and outlook, and little exposed to trends in urban centers. Hugo might have met adept photographers in St. Louis or Memphis, but the Arkansas Delta was hardly an epicenter of photographic advancement. Here, there were no photography salons as on the East and West coasts and in Europe, and thus, Gayne's art developed in a vacuum. Her isolation makes it unfair to purposefully compare her work to her peers. She created in an insular world, not influenced by any working photographer directly. Though she cut out portraits in popular magazines, especially pictorial fashion portraits in natural settings, she likely did not see photographic journals like

Gayne Preller perused magazines and collected cutouts of poses. In this exquisite fashion-influenced picture, she utilized textured backdrops and perfectly articulated natural light from an open window.

Alfred Stieglitz's *CameraWork*, nor work by photographic modernists in Europe during the 1920s. There were no pilgrimages to New York or San Francisco to attend shows and she did not work under a guiding spirit like a Weston or Käsebier.

Unlike many early photographers, Gayne's work is not divisible into periods that roughly correspond to breakthroughs in photographic equipment and technique. She never experiments with form, shadow or texture like Stieglitz and Weston. She never pursues a portfolio of themed images, like "hard times" or "sharecroppers" and the like. One finds no experimental prints that utilize montage, solarization, photograms, mirrors, unique light modifiers, nor the combining of photographic prints with oil or watercolor painting, other than the early use of retouching inks. All of these techniques one might have expected to see, given that her husband was a painter. She stubbornly travels her own path, her photographic style and approach changing little over the half century that she worked. She focused on what her equipment could produce quickly for a willing customer. When asked what was fascinating for her about portraiture, Imogen Cunningham once exclaimed, "Money!...it's simply a livelihood." I think Gayne Preller would have agreed.

Keeping It Simple. Nearly all of her portraits were made using natural light and long exposures. Often the subject is blurred due to movement while the shutter was open; relatively few of the images are pin sharp. The light sensitivity of glass negatives was the equivalent of ISO 10-25, meaning that her exposures had to be at least one-fifteenth of a second inside the studio. Children are usually blurred since they seldom freeze for long. Probably this was frustrating to Gayne, to shoot and develop a negative only to see a fuzzy image in the fixing bath. But she wasn't looking for technical perfection. Though she was a fastidious printer, running test print after test print in search of strong tonality, foremost she was seeking good composition and expression. In truth, the rawness, the routine use of similar backdrops, even the random fixer stains, lend a patina of authenticity to her work—an aura of lost treasure discovered.

What Gayne lacked in technique was compensated by the poignancy of her pictures, which are unvarnished and simple. Much of their warmth and magic comes from the background and drop rug that provided depth and texture. When these

All of the ingredients of a classic Preller picture are here: the top-down natural light, smart styling, fun use of props, and foreground and background backdrops to add depth and texture.

disappear in her 1940s work, her photographs become objective, if not antiseptic, much like Mike Disfarmer's work from the same period. Gayne's technique remained unrefined but practical. Her aesthetic aimed to depict people at ease, presenting their best aspect. Knowing her limitations in both technique and in time, she produced salable images well presented, and left the art world to its own devices. The sitter came first. And this is the charm of the collection; it is sincere and devoid of cynicism or political viewpoint. Gayne Preller was her own person, under the guiding influence of no one, except perhaps her god.

"The Executive," by Gayne Preller, circa 1940.

These are original door panels from the Preller's House of Doors in Augusta, Arkansas. The backdrop was originally painted by Hugo Preller and was used most in Preller portraits. *This facsimile was painted by artist Mary Kern.*

A
House of Doors

After settling in Augusta, Arkansas, the Preller's purchased a "House of Doors" from Sears and Roebuck. This was a popular mail-order house constructed of wooden panels. The Prellers later expanded their home and store by attaching an identical unit; Hugo's watch and gun repair shop was on the left side, while Gayne's studio and store were on the right. The Preller Variety Shop was a community landmark for almost 50 years.

Pictured on the left are four of the original door panels from the House of Doors once located on Second Street in Augusta. The painted backdrop is a facsimile of one that Hugo created, and Gayne used most, during the early 1900s. The wicker sitting chair that appears in many Preller portraits is still owned by Gayne Preller Schmidt and sits in the window of her dress shop today.

A small darkroom stood adjacent to the studio space where Mrs. Preller processed negatives and prints. Gayne never stopped using a large-format view camera in the studio. She photographed using only natural light controlled by opening and closing windows and a skylight. As trends changed, she chose not to use artificial flash nor shoot in color.

She closed the shop in 1952, as demand slackened and consumer photography grew. In 1973, photographer-historian Greer Lile purchased the House of Doors and had it dismantled and shipped to his photography museum in Little Rock. The rebuilding of it there became problematic and he returned it to the Preller family in the 1980s. In 2013, as part of this project, we retrieved and restored some of the original panels and included them in the *House of Light* exhibition.

Downtown Augusta, Arkansas, circa 1910. This glass negative was made by Hugo Preller and is inscribed with his distinctive lettering.
Photo courtesy of the University of Central Arkansas Archive.

Painting with Light In a One-Horse Town

The Prellers had been living on the water for nearly a decade. They had eked out a living and prospered, yet four Preller children had died young due to illness and accidents. Adventurous as riverboat residency was, the romance of it must have worn thin, especially for Gayne. One can imagine how the family would have yearned to put down roots on dry land. Augusta, in the cotton-rich Arkansas Delta, was the perfect spot, with a new church and school, and located on the elevated east side of the majestic White River. The Prellers built their house on a lot they purchased at the end of Second Street in Augusta, near the library

The House of Doors as it stood in Augusta in 1973. This is the right half of the Preller building; the left half was two stories high and connected with a veranda. *Photo courtesy of Greer Lile.*

and across from the wood-frame Hinton House, one of the few structures on the east end of town. Around the corner was the Post Office and not 100 yards away was the high bank of the river.

There is no solid evidence as to the origin of the house they built in Augusta. All that we know is that they called it "the house of doors," and that Sears and Roebuck sold a range of prefabricated homes starting at that time.

Greer Lile remembers how it was constructed and compared it to the Preller floating gallery. He told me the house was constructed much like the Preller's houseboat studio had been. "If you look down the boat's side," Greer explained, (see the photo on page 41), "you get an idea of how the studio and repair shop were built. There was a 2-by-12 that they stood on edge, and it had a one-inch groove along the top. And this ran around the entire length of the building. You had a series of doors that fit into the groove. And that's where Hugo got the idea. They stood the doors in the slot and screwed them to the 2-by-12, and then the next door slid in. They used a straight piece of metal to

In an endearing picture by Hugo Preller, the "coming lights of Augusta" are posed in front of the bay window of the Preller Variety Shop, circa 1910. At magnification, one can see in the window a number of framed pictures and a guitar that appears in some Preller portraits. Victor Preller II is on the right.

hold them together. And there was a canvas roof—canvas over wood. I tore that thing off myself," remembers Greer.

Whether Sears supplied the house or not, the door panels were prefabricated and assembled by the Prellers. Later, the family added an identical unit next door and built a second story on top. The single surviving picture of the Preller Variety Shop in business depicts a group of children lined up in front of the bay window.

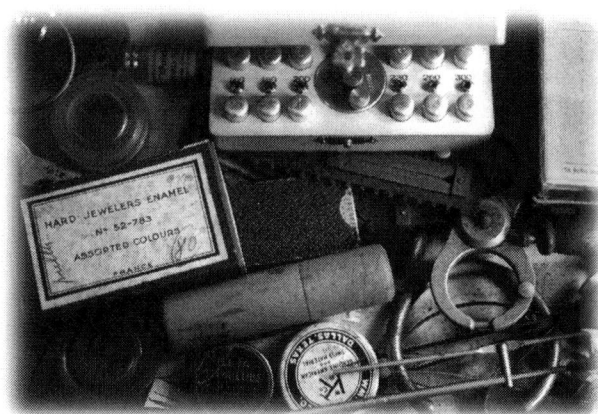

Miniature tools and tiny watch parts found in Hugo's jeweler's desk, at which he spent most of his working hours in intense concentration.

The year is 1910 and the left side of the building has not yet been added. Hugo inscribed the photograph, "The Coming Lights of Augusta," referring to the promising youths he pictured. Since no photograph showing its interior survives, we must imagine the inside of the Preller Variety Shop, with Gayne's refined feminine good taste creating a warm and social atmosphere.

In 1946, the Preller's eldest son, Victor II, established a TV repair shop located directly across the street from the House of Doors, and which Preller descendants operated until 2012.

Inside the House of Doors

Beaming with excitement, five-year-old Gayne Preller (Victor II's daughter) would cross the narrow street from her father's TV repair shop to the House of Doors. Hugo's street sign, painted on a huge wooden pocket watch, hung from the veranda on the left. On the right, Gayne's store had no sign, but her bay window brimmed with curios and photographs. A bell rang as little Gayne entered the door of the shop. Her grandmother would appear with a smile wearing an ankle-length cotton dress—"an everyday dress," says Gayne Schmidt, now 83 and living in Augusta. "She wore her hair in a knot and had a collection of the fanciest combs I'd ever seen. She wore a curved hairpin, some with jewels on the end."

Then in his seventies, Hugo Preller would be sitting on his side of the shop behind a lattice screen that kept customers and children away from his special tools and guns, hunched over his miniature work wearing an eyepiece magnifier. "Don't bother your grandfather," Mrs. Preller would say to the young girl. "He's working." The year is 1940 and Mrs. Preller is over 60 years old but she moves quickly. She grabs little Gayne and plops her on the sitting chair. "She always wanted me on that stool to get my picture taken," says Ms. Schmidt. When a little older, her grandmother would then ask, "You feel like going to the post office?" and she'd hand the girl a bundle of letters and print orders. "She'd give me a quarter to walk a block to mail things, and a quarter was a bunch of money in 1947." After that, Mrs. Preller would shuffle the child to the upright piano in a back room and listen with undivided attention while she played her latest lesson. (Hugo played the violin and Gayne Preller had studied piano from adolescence.) "Grandma offered me five dollars if I would learn *Faust*," says Ms. Schmidt. She also encouraged her granddaughter to learn portrait photography, telling her, "it was a good business."

Young Gayne was permitted to remain in the shop when customers came in. Her grandmother would strike up a conversation with visitors instantly, but she wasn't a hard sell.

An advertisement for a Kodak Autograph collapsible camera from the early 1900s. In the studio, the Prellers used a bulky view camera mounted on a wooden tripod, but for outdoor work and candid shots, they used a portable roll film camera like this one.

"When people walked through her door they were part of the family," Ms. Schmidt recalls. "Everyone loved her." She would show visitors the new things she had collected and placed in her glass cases—pins, cards, ceramics, and beautiful stationary. And she had catalogs from everywhere laid out on the marble tabletops for visitors to browse. "She was engaging with clients so they would be comfortable and bright-faced for their pictures."

Mrs. Preller would invite her granddaughter to stand behind her and under the black cloth that covered her view camera. "I could see the little upside-down picture on the back of the camera," Ms. Schmidt says. "The skylight was directly above the shooting area, and light entered from the front window too." Mrs. Preller did not use umbrellas or flood lights (though the house had electricity), and hence, she only shot during the day. One of several painted backdrops on rollers could be drawn down to provide a background. After Mrs. Preller squeezed a bulb to release the shutter, her granddaughter would often accompany her to the darkroom where, in total darkness, the film was removed from the camera back and developed in enameled trays. Films were then hung on a clothesline to dry. A little curtained window looked out on the studio, with a red safety light just above. To make prints, a dried

The G. S. Woodson Company in Memphis was an important photographic supplier in the region. The year is 1901 and the Preller's have ordered supplies from Columbus, Kentucky, further evidence that they returned to Kentucky after living in Memphis during the last years of the 1800s.

negative was loaded into a wooden contact-printing box and exposed, probably with natural light entering the peep window. In the dim glow of the safelight, the two Gayne's would gaze expectantly as the image magically appeared in the porcelain tray.

How the Prellers Made Pictures

When the Prellers began to make pictures in 1895, photography had only existed for fifty years. Unlike professional portrait painting, the new industry of photographic portraiture (as is the case today) required little, if any, formal artistic or technical training of the practitioner. This was surely one reason for the "instant" growth of the new industry. The sudden emergence of an inexpensive, easy-to-learn art form was a boon especially to women seeking job opportunities. Many studios routinely hired female assistants and some were operated solely by artistic and entrepreneurial female proprietors. By 1900, the industry employed thousands of women in American cities and many in the countryside as well. Film was not yet invented, so photographers made pictures by applying light-sensitive silver to a metal or glass surface.

The earliest Preller images are called *tintypes*, which are one-of-a-kind pictures made on metal. The process was cumbersome and, like the earlier *daguerreotype*, the tintype could not be reproduced on paper. It is possible that the Prellers also made pictures using *wet plates*, a process that required coating glass with toxic chemicals and then exposing the plate while it was still wet.

With the advent of *dry glass plates* in the late 1800s, photography became simpler and more accessible to the hobbyist and professional alike. Using dry plates, Gayne Preller made her first pictures as a teenager, and by the time she and Hugo were married, pre-sensitized dry plates could be purchased by mail. Glass negative images are durable and can be reproduced using a process called contact printing. The plate was placed atop a sheet of paper that had been pre-coated with gelatin silver. Sunlight was allowed to pass through the plate and cast an image onto the paper. After exposure, the paper was processed with chemicals like the glass plate had been. The process took less than 30 minutes and multiple prints could be made. Most important, a glass negative image could be reproduced with no degradation of quality.

A glass negative made in the Preller studio, depicting Victor Preller II and an attractive friend. Only twenty such glass plates survive in printable condition in the collection. On the right, the image has been inverted to show what a print would look like.

Though Kodak offered a portable film camera as of the late 1880s, most professional studio photographers continued to use bulky view cameras loaded with glass plates. Some sent their plates to a lab to be processed and printed, while others, like Gayne and Hugo, purchased Kodak chemicals or mixed their own, and undertook their own processing. While Gayne used a view camera in the studio, Hugo used a portable film camera outdoors; the Prellers could be hired to make impromptu portraits and group pictures, and they also covered events like the building of a railroad line or the blasting of forest land to prepare it for farming. The Prellers were unique in that they also offered photo enlargements, not just contact prints limited to the size of the original glass plate. To make an enlargement, a darkroom must be equipped with an enlarger that projects light through the negative onto a sheet of photo paper at a desired magnification. It is not known what enlarger the Prellers used, but it must have been one of the earliest available in the South.

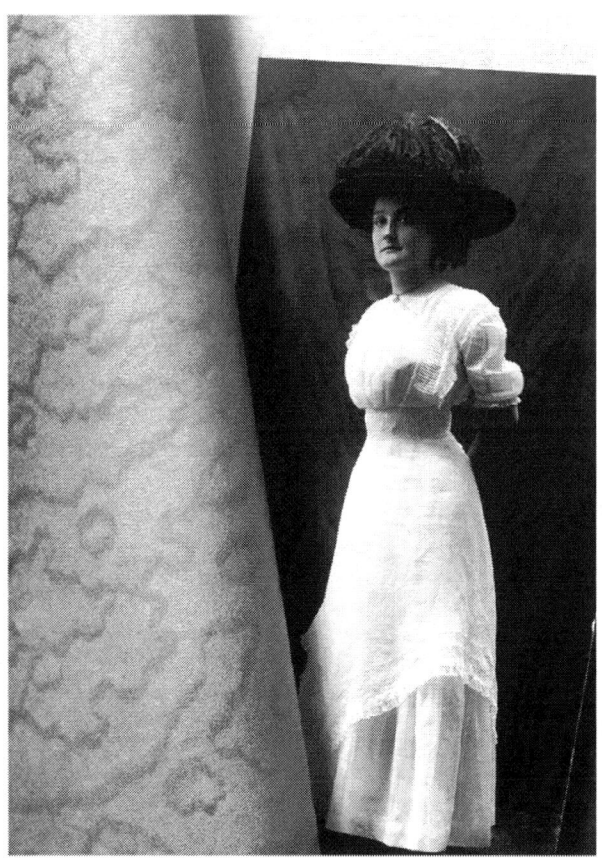

Only a few Preller prints in the collection are cabinet card enlargements. This wonderful full-body portrait has been printed and mounted on textured cardboard, with an attractive foil coverlet added for protection.

An Explosion of Photographic Media

As making pictures became simpler and less expensive, public demand for images exploded. A wave of new paper media flooded the market—cards, calendars and prints—as people used photographic images to document their lives and record events. This photographic renaissance was the biggest development in mass media until the arrival of television 50 years later.

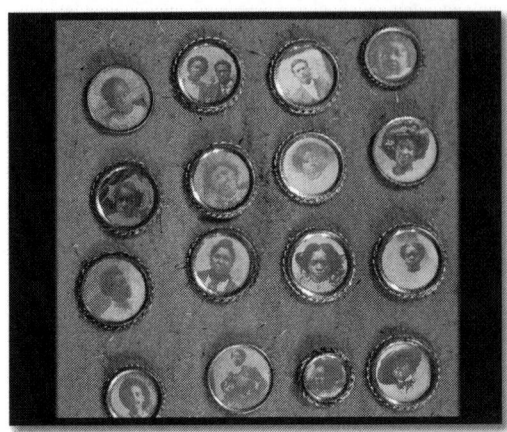

All of the memorial buttons in *The Preller Collection* depict African Americans and only one person pictured has been identified, in a portrait made in 1908.

Popular Prints. By the turn of the 20th century, the typical family in America was familiar with a host of photographic print formats. Starting in 1887, paper contact prints from glass negatives were pasted onto card stock and called *cabinet cards*. Portraits were typically formal in pose and lighting, and sometimes they were embellished with colored ink applied by a trained hand. Their elegance could be enhanced with a thin tissue coverlet and decorative printed filigree on the mat board. They were usually placed in a glass cabinet or on a shelf in the home.

The *carte de visité* was a smaller image of 2 ½ x 4 inches and was contact printed onto pre-printed paper with a place for a stamp and mailing address on the rear side. These popular "post card" photographs were purchased and distributed by people around the world, the first instance of mass image sharing.

Sometimes called *penny pictures*, a small-sized portrait could be inserted into a wearable pin. Among African Americans in Woodruff County, Arkansas where the Prellers worked, these so-called memorial buttons were popular, worn in remembrance of a friend or family member after their passing. *The Preller Collection* includes over 100 such buttons, most created in the early 1900s. **Humorous Pictures.** An important early, but often overlooked, genre of image making was the comical photograph. Both of the Prellers could be zany and were always willing to camp it up in front of the camera. They weren't shy in offering clients a visual pun or pastiche. Hugo's illustration was often included in these, which blended his absurdist perspective with Southern-style corniness (see "A Slow Race," on the next page).

A Community Fixture

By the coming of the Great Depression, the Prellers were considered old timers in Augusta, having been in business there for 20 years. The Preller Variety Shop had become a landmark and its reputation reached beyond Woodruff County. The Prellers had raised four boys, all of whom inherited their parent's intelligence, artistic talent, and traditional values. Hard times were to come for the South, but the Prellers fared better than the great majority due to the diversity of services that they offered and their bonhomie with community members.

Lodged in a briar patch on family property for over 30 years, the House of Doors awaits resurrection. Unfortunately, only a few of the over 50 weathered panels could be restored and put on display.

Hugo Preller created a host of whimsical drawings and cartoon style backdrops; this one is a montage featuring Gayne Preller in "A Slow Race."

But while the Preller saga might sound like a fairy tale, the family faced its share of adversity. Four of eight children did not survive the age of four years of age. One child was accidentally poisoned while two others died from illnesses. And Max, their third son to survive, experienced an unfortunate event during adolescence that altered his life permanently.

One morning he was behind the counter with his dad in the House of Doors. A local man they knew came in to see a Civil War-era rifle that hung on the wall. He had come in before to ask about the same gun. As the Prellers knew the fellow to be a town drunk, they treated him with caution. But without warning, the man suddenly leaped over the glass counter and pulled the rifle from the wall. Hugo jumped up and took hold of the man and the gun barrel. But in his attempt to get the weapon free, the assailant began to club Hugo with the rifle. Young Max grabbed a pistol from the wall, and when the man ran outside the store with the rifle, Max was in pursuit. A moment later a gunshot rang out on the next block. The intruder lay dead and Max held the pistol.

It's impossible to know what motivated Max to give chase and shoot the man. Ms. Schmidt believes that he might have felt the man had mortally injured his father. In the months that followed, Max became increasingly troubled by his action. He consulted

> "One of the very interesting places in Augusta is with Mr. and Mrs. G. L. Preller. They are among our old timers who have been here when things were booming on the river and they have been here during the lean period which followed. Their place on Second Street was in the past, and is today one of great interest to visit. Mr. Preller is known far and wide for his watch and jewelry repair work and Mrs. Preller for her interesting studio. She has a collection of pictures both new and old which she has taken well worth going to see."
>
> Arkansas Advocate
> September 12, 1929

Scripture, seeking to justify the taking of a man's life, but he could find no such justification, and over time became introverted and depressed. The family sought help but nothing stopped his decline. Soon, a boy with such promise was wandering the streets and committing petty crimes. In the end, Max had to be institutionalized and lived separately from the family until Mrs. Preller's last years when she insisted that Max move back in with her. "But that did not work out very well," recalls Ms. Schmidt, as Max continued to get into trouble in town, like the time he returned home with someone else's chickens. Max would live in a mental health institution for the rest of his life.

Gayne Preller operated the studio until 1952, two years after Hugo's death. Later, her grandson Minnert opened a donut shop in the building. By 1973, the House of Doors was listing toward the public library next door. At that time, Little Rock photographer and historian Greer Lile made arrangements with Gayne Preller Schmidt to purchase the building and reconstruct it on the grounds of his photography museum. "With the help of Augusta's mayor, I got a crew together and took the guys over to the hardware store," recalled Mr. Lile in 2013. "And I said to them, 'Boys, pick out the tools you'll need. And when you're all through, these are your tools to keep.' They were all so excited, but there was a method in this, as they weren't going to *lose* those tools. And during the job, nobody lost a single tool."

Greer's crew took apart the House of Doors and numbered the panels for reassembly. The windows did not survive. "There was one guy who just couldn't keep a sheet of glass in the frame," recalls Greer. "Every window he touched broke to pieces. It was just weird..." So today, we don't have the building's bay window display that you see in the photographs on page 68.

Unfortunately, Greer's plans to rebuild the Preller Variety Shop were not to be. "It sat out here for eight years," he says at his museum in Little Rock. "I didn't have the time or the money to do what I had planned with it." His son, Brett, believes now that the House of Doors should have stayed in Augusta, and both he and his father are happy to learn that, after Greer returned the panels to Augusta in the early1980s, our team located a number of them under an oak tree on Preller family land in 2013. In fact, I had ten of the original panels stacked on top of my SUV when I arrived for our visit. Greer's face lit up in disbelief.

"So," his son Brett exclaimed, "the House of Doors has been full circle twice!"

When Greer took down the Preller home and studio, the only photographic item he found inside was a single glass negative of the Preller's floating studio. Much of the Preller's memorabilia had been burned when the house was cleaned out after Hugo and Gayne passed away. Although the Preller archive contains over 2,400 images, this is only a part of the original collection. Ms. Schmidt recounts a terrible day when she found family members casting drawers filled with papers and prints onto a pyre outside of the House of Doors. She demanded that they stop immediately, yet a vast cache of memorabilia and negatives was lost. On the bright side, in 2013, after the passing of her brother, Ms. Schmidt successfully retrieved Hugo Preller's jeweler's desk packed with his 100-year-old tools and watch parts.

Inside Greer Lile's photography museum in Little Rock, his son, Brett, displays a model of the Preller's floating gallery, which Mr. Lile built in the 1970s after purchasing the House of Doors in Augusta.

A family reunion photographed by the Prellers around 1900, probably near Gayne Preller's hometown of Columbus, Kentucky.

Faith In Community

As economic downturn, world war and racial hatred tore at the fabric of society in the South in the first half of the 20th century, the Prellers never lost faith in their community. Even after being ostracized during World War II due to Hugo's German background, and witnessing racial discrimination in their midst, their work consistently honored all members of the Delta family.

While African Americans living in their area were forced to ride at the back of a bus and could be punished if they tried to enter a 'white' train car or restroom, all people were welcome in the Preller portrait studio and rendered with absolute equality. Gayne's studio remained an inviting stage upon which the taboos and conventions of Jim Crow were only a distant madness.

As her granddaughter remembers: "Gayne Preller was color blind." Augusta's elders recall her good taste, great conversation and acceptance of everyone.

Gayne's portraits of African Americans speak for themselves. Nothing is known about the sitters other than what we can glean from the images, as none of these pictures is inscribed with names or dates. All of their subjects exude poignant secrets but we are deaf in their midst. How did they learn about the Preller studio? Where did their children go to school? Were they sharecroppers on farms nearby? We may never know. All that we know is what we feel looking at the individuals and guessing at what Gayne Preller felt while making their portraits.

The Preller's African-American Portraits

Well into the process of archiving the collection, up in a damp attic above Ms. Schmidt's dress shop, two long-forgotten boxes full of photographs were discovered. The Prellers had become important businesspeople in the community, and people came from all over the region to be photographed by them, including African Americans whom they photographed with great artistry. Over 400 of the roughly 1,800 Preller studio portraits that survive, depict African Americans, most made in the early 1900s. This unique body of work represents a fascinating aspect of the collection in light of the history of tenant farming and the battle for civil rights in the South. Looking at these portraits, it appears that all people felt comfortable in the Preller studio, relaxed, and with their guard lowered.

On display in this Preller snapshot are a few of the well understood social cues prevalent during the Jim Crow era in the South. White children stand tall while an African American man – who likely worked for the family – keeps his distance.

Racial Reality In the Delta

The Preller's lives roughly coincide with the life of so-called Jim Crow law in the South. Named after a character in a minstrel show, historians and sociologists use the term "Jim Crow" to refer to the customs and laws that discriminated against African Americans until the civil-rights struggle brought an end to segregation in the 1960s. These rules set out to manage how African American and Anglo-Saxon people would live, work and interact with each other in Post-Reconstruction America. Each state enforced its own variation of the customary rules and ratified laws, yet their common purpose was to ensure that African Americans were separated, treated differently, and barred from public areas where white people congregated, including restaurants, churches, hotels, restrooms and public transportation. A "Whites Only" sign became the grim emblem of the era. A blacks-only train car was called a Jim Crow car.

Could Jim Crow laws be applied to a photo studio? Was is possible that, in Augusta, a sheriff could stroll by the Preller Variety Shop and insist that African Americans enter through a back door or use a separate sitting chair than the light-complexioned clients? Ms. Schmidt says that her grandparents would have had no patience for such nonsense. I ask her about what she remembers of the Jim Crow years in Augusta:

An album of original portraits of African Americans was lent to a friend of the family years before research began on this book, and thankfully, returned intact.

"Do you recall the community being divided racially when you were a young girl?"

"Whites here were very proud, and the blacks reluctantly knew their place," Ms. Schmidt recalls. "There was no violence that I can remember, but there was an understanding."

I ask: "Were there 'whites-only' signs in restaurants or restrooms that separated the races?"

"I only saw whites-only signs in Memphis, not in Augusta," Ms. Schmidt says. "The N-word was used here in town, but not in my family."

Ms. Schmidt remembers her grandmother's open and egalitarian attitude, and how "some parties in town might not have agreed with her." Given their life experience, it's easy to

appreciate how Hugo and Gayne would possess a progressive attitude concerning race that many whites in Augusta might not have shared. Perhaps idealizing the couple's sensibility, I considered the possibility of whether Mrs. Preller had made it a personal project to seek out people of color as a photographic project. Why else would there be so many pictures of African Americans in *The Preller Collection*? I surmised that, like her contemporary, Imogen Cunningham, Gayne might have pictured people she sensed would soon otherwise be forgotten, "honoring the other" by preserving them in pictures. My faulty logic went even further: perhaps Mrs. Preller offered her services as a charity to some of these families.

Of course, I had fallen headlong into a stereotyping trap. I listened again carefully to a recorded interview in which Ms. Schmidt and I talked about her childhood in Augusta during in the 1940s.

I asked her then: "As a child visiting the House of Doors, did black people come into the shop?"

"Oh yes. Everyone was welcome there."

"So African American families would arrive to have portraits made?"

"Yes, often."

"There was nothing special about the fact that they had come in, as if Gayne Preller had arranged for them to be pictured?"

"No. They lived in the community and they wanted pictures made. Many of them were sharecroppers and lived in tenant houses along the highway, near McCrory, Gregory, on out to Cotton Plant."

Clearly, photographing African Americans was not a "project" for Mrs. Preller; she didn't seek out African Americans in a journalistic impulse to document rural poverty. They were regular customers.

Saturday In the Delta

I arranged to speak with Ms. Schmidt again to revisit this topic.

As her recollections crystalized, she told me about what Saturdays were like in Augusta when she was growing up. As in most Delta towns, farming families rode into town on that day from every direction on "buckboard" wagons to shop and have some fun. Four thousand people lived in Augusta then, and on Saturday afternoon, the main street would be packed with

As in all interracial Preller photographs, whites and blacks have separated themselves in this view of a train engine team in Augusta, Arkansas, circa 1915.

automobiles and wagons, and the out-of-towners who arrived in them.

"My grandmother didn't make appointments and she had no phone," Ms. Schmidt begins. "So people came into Augusta to have their portraits made. The African Americans came to town on Saturday. They mainly worked as tenant farmers on the cotton and bean farms near town, and besides shopping for groceries and farm supplies, many wanted their pictures taken, too." While one group was getting their pictures done, she says, another group would be waiting outside the shop. "I was told to sit and wait and not bother my grandfather while he worked."

She remembers out-of-town visitors crowding around the glass curio cases and looking over Mrs. Preller's baskets, needlework, hairpins, and other knickknacks.

"A Saturday was my grandmother's best day," she recalls. "I would guess that eighty percent of the original photographs in the collection were made on Saturdays."

Now I understood. The town filled with visitors on Saturday, many of whom were African-American farm workers and their families. And this day was Mrs. Preller's most active, and probably her most lucrative. The upshot was that her photographing African Americans was no liberal-arts project, but was bread and butter for the business. And, of course, this explained the large number of African-American portraits in the collection.

An African-American civic organization likely commissioned the Prellers to make this picture around 1915. Gayne used a pair of American flags (48 stars) as a backdrop here and in a number of other portraits.

But in light of what I had learned about Jim Crow laws and social taboos, I could not imagine the Preller's studio on Saturdays. I asked Ms. Schmidt: "Would African Americans and white people be in the store together, or waiting on the porch together?" She hesitated while she visualized being in the House of Doors as an adolescent in the early 1940s. She said: "Come to think of it, I don't recall blacks and whites being there at the same time. The whites lived in town and they came in on weekdays." Needless to say, race relations were uneasy in Augusta even at the Preller studio. Though Mrs. Preller was welcoming to all, and African Americans represented an important clientele, the social mores of the times enforced rules of interaction over which Mrs. Preller would have little influence.

Picturing Jim Crow

Whatever might have been the social climate in town, African Americans were photographed inside the House of Doors exactly as white people were, without the slightest difference imparted by the photographer. While inequality was enforced outside, in Preller images we see *equality* visualized inside the studio. Everyone is pictured against the same backdrop, in the same sitting chairs, with the same props. A sort of leveling imbues the style of the portraits that transcends race and class. These are Gayne Preller's customers and fellow citizens; they are not "apart" as African Americans were often imaged during this

period.

    The Preller's pictures of African Americans test some of our impressions of the era and validate others. Foremost, we find an unexpected diversity among the African Americans pictured. A rural farming couple, hats in hand. A pair of well-dressed sisters holding textbooks, presumedly excited about their education. A sophisticated gentleman wearing a fine suit striking a distinguished pose between puffs on a cigar. Yet there are telling

differences to be recognized in the images. Unlike her typical white sitters, the African Americans whom Gayne pictured tend to look stoic and gloomy. There are no games or frolic. Their eyes are globes of something other than joy. Bodies often limp. Clothes sometimes drab and ill fitting. But there is respect on the photographer's part—an ennobling sincerity and attention to detail.

White men clearly wanted to be pictured *doing something* in their pictures—engaged in physical or intellectual action, and often in uniform. A man sits in communion with his newspaper, discerning the events of the day. Two boys raise gloved fists, mimicking a boxing match. A city elder dons a dress as part of a Red Cross community event. African-American men behave differently before the lens; they are inward-looking and stare at the camera (at Mrs. Preller) with little or no expression. They appear less sure of themselves and do not smile. In over 200 pictures, there are not more than two instances of an African-American man smiling for the camera. Clearly many sitters were challenged trying to survive as tenant farmers. It's also plain that some of them were undernourished, especially the children.

But there is nothing patronizing in these photographs. Unlike WPA photography, they don't depict "downtrodden" minority citizens and they don't single out desperate individuals and make them symbols or ideas promoting social reform. Gayne does not depict racism, which many of these sitters would have experienced. She depicts relationships—between two brothers, two sisters, between a farming couple and between African American individuals and themselves. In portraying personalities rather than a political viewpoint, she subtly renders the effects of brutal servitude embodied in the sharecropper system. The sitters are not trying to hide their hardship; they are caught in the act of putting their best face forward, regardless of their plight. By not asking them to "smile," she emphasizes their dignity.

Unfortunately, all-too-few Preller pictures depict the sinister workings of Jim Crow in the public space—the apartness, forced servility and expectation of obedience.

However, at the few interracial gatherings that the Prellers did record, African Americans stand apart from whites usually to the rear and/or to the side of the camera view. One wonders if they were included in the view by accident, and whether the whites were even privy to their inclusion in the photo. Hugo Preller can be credited with making these photographs. A family reunion photo (on page 82) is perhaps the most revealing group portrait made by the Prellers. We see an extended family of whites, and African-American young men standing in the background. They appear to be teenagers, well dressed for the occasion. What role did they play in the family? Where are their parents? What were they paid?

The Preller's Egalitarian Values

How would have Hugo and Gayne acquired an inclusive attitude about race, which was not likely shared by many of the whites in their photographs? Simply put, the Prellers exposure to cultural diversity would have set them apart from the typical Augustan. Their enlightened perspective would have been forged by many influences, including Hugo's outlook as an immigrant, their experience living on the river, and by racial turmoil, especially in Memphis, that they would have heard about or witnessed first hand.

They had been itinerant artists and lived on five American rivers at the turn of the 20th century. One can imagine the crazy quilt of diverse souls that comprised river society along these banks. This was a tight-knit, multiracial community always threatened by weather and flood. Many African Americans and American Indians lived on or near the river alongside white people like the Prellers and worked side-by-side them. Hugo and Gayne would have known African-American fishers, trappers and mussel-shell harvesters, who, like the Prellers, lived in vulnerable houseboats moored in inlets and bays, living on the edge of survival every day.

The river and its elements are a great equalizer and leave little room for putting on airs about one's social status or ethnicity.

"The Student," portrait by Gayne Preller, circa 1910.

When the river floods, everyone's palace is a mud-filled wreck. River life levels people, and the Preller's egalitarian sensibility would have been annealed by living on it. Moreover, as in recent times, there existed an unwritten law of the river that could not be ignored. The long arm of the law was hardly long enough to reach the river bottoms. Law and order was enforced by a code that put the river's residents on an equal footing—if you did someone wrong, you could expect the deed to be avenged. "River justice" is the common term for it in the Delta, even today. The system didn't usually play favorites based on race, as was the case all too often in mainstream America.

Gayne Preller had likely become comfortable with a mixed-race crowd early in life at her father's mercantile store. A sale was a sale, no matter the color of the customer's skin. Her parents were Southerners but not Delta people, probably closer in mentality to the northern states than the Deep South. Hugo and Gayne Preller were all but immigrants when they arrived in the deep Delta, not weaned in the Cotton Kingdom and quite unlike the stereotypical white southerner of the era in social perspective. And Hugo, of course, was European and harbored none of the negative attitudes toward African Americans that marked many underemployed southern whites during Reconstruction and after. Gayne would have been influenced by Hugo's émigré outlook, which was highly appreciative of the independence and resourcefulness of the river rats and hill folk with whom they would have rubbed elbows.

Hugo was also a devout Christian who studied, and lived Biblical philosophy. Gayne wasn't a proselytizer like him, but they both were active and conservative Methodists—prizing honesty, mutual respect and good manners. ("Do unto others as you would have them do unto you.") Though they were hardly activists for social causes, I believe any public display of bigotry would have disturbed them both deeply.

The Prellers traversed a region undergoing a long healing process after the Civil War, where cleavages between past and present persisted. Nowhere was this more the case than in

Memphis, where they lived and worked intermittently from 1892 to 1905. In the few decades since the end of the Civil War, freedmen had flocked there to harvest cotton, work the docks, and open shops. The Memphis economy prospered, skyscrapers rose and black success stories were well publicized. African-American culture took root in the Beale Street District and many African

Americans achieved prominence. But it was also an era when ghastly lynchings reached their peak. In Memphis, an event occurred with which the Prellers would have been familiar. While they were residents of the city, white racists publicly murdered three prominent African-American mercantile storeowners. Like many who lived in Memphis, the Prellers would have been shocked that such violent animus could have followed the Civil War that abolished slavery.

The Community Turns on the Prellers

For forty years, the Prellers had been well liked and respected in Augusta, and so it is bitterly ironic that they would fall victim to ethnic hatred themselves, ostracized when the community turned on Hugo Preller due to his Germanic background. When the Nazis invaded Europe, anti-German sentiment flared in Woodruff County. Gayne Schmidt remembers how she and her brother were jeered at by other schoolchildren for having German ancestry. The big blow was to 75-year-old Hugo when his beloved church barred him from teaching Sunday school any longer. He felt the sting deeply and began seeking out another church, even travelling to Michigan to visit with the Isrealite House of David, which he considered joining though nothing more is known. Ironically, during the rise of Nazism in Germany, Hugo expressed his concern and suspicion about Adolf Hitler to his sister-in-law in an exchange of letters with her in 1938. She lived in Berlin and operated a factory there making kid gloves (which she closed down in 1938 for unknown reasons) and wrote to Hugo describing her patriotic support for der Führer, praising what he was doing to reclaim respect for the Fatherland. She was aghast that Hugo remained skeptical.

Something else was happening, too. Hugo's mission in life had been, as he articulated it, "to know the truth" about man's origin and purpose, and indeed, his own. His spiritual quest demanded that he question Scripture, but his fellow community members were not accommodating when he began to question Church doctrine. He laments the situation vigorously in an unpublished manuscript:

> When I chose [not] to adhere closely to the commands and injunctions of the Bible, and to leave cut and dried creeds and accepted beliefs...by which I might be led into a higher knowledge of the truth...then [I was] at once confronted with a radical change on the part of those who once professed love and friendship as Christian coworkers and church members and followers of Jesus Christ....Dare to differ with those around you and to leave the beaten path of orthodox creeds....And at once you stand alone, become a subject of derision, are branded a fool, and fanatic.

Hugo kept to himself more and more during these years. Moreover, he was hindered by spinal arthritis, restricted to the use of short crutches on which he hobbled about town. One of his activities, from which he derived therapeutic benefit, was to propel himself down to the White River landing in Augusta where he would doff his crutches and enter the current to swim around the bend to The Narrows (see map). There, he'd grasp the shore and crawl through the woods to the river about 100 yards

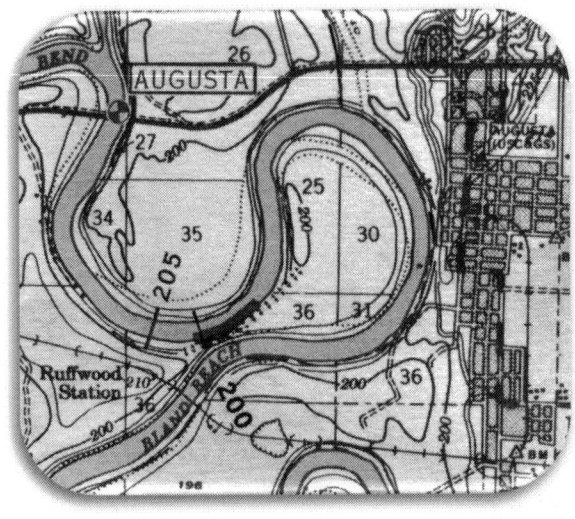

The town of Augusta, Arkansas sits on an extreme meander in the White River about 200 miles from the river's mouth. Locals call the 100-yard-wide spit of land that divides the river (along Bland Reach) The Narrows. A trestle crosses the river just downstream and remains in use today. *Map source: Army Corps of Engineers.*

across, where he'd reenter the stream and float back into town. The course was roughly two miles and he completed it often. More than once, Mrs. Preller got an urgent message from someone who thought they had seen a body floating in the White River, and asked if Hugo was okay.

Gayne Preller would be saddened by the state of race relations in Augusta today. Sitting recently in the Methodist church that Hugo and Gayne attended, I noticed that not one African American was sitting in the pews of the nearly full church. Perhaps the African Americans in the community, who make up sixty percent of its residents, were mostly Baptists. Then suddenly, as if reading my thoughts, the pastor, Robert DeBaun, bellowed an admonishment to his congregation: "We are a *divided* community..." and he complained that his congregation was stubbornly split along racial lines. Later I learned that the Augusta area has two Methodist churches located not two miles apart. One serves a congregation entirely of white people, while the other serves one solely comprised of African Americans. Gayne Schmidt, who has chaired Augusta's Chamber of Commerce in the past, explained to me that an African American owns not one of Augusta's twenty businesses on the main street, and only one member of the Chamber is an African American.

* * *

Like the river, the years drifted by. Augusta's halcyon days faded and the rural population of the Delta dwindled with the arrival of farm automation. After being bedridden in the House of Doors for two years, Hugo died in 1950 at the age of 85. Gayne Preller operated the shop for two more years, and in 1955, passed away at age 80, in the care of her family in Augusta. The year before, the Supreme Court decision on Brown vs. Board of Education heralded the end of legal segregation in America and the swansong of Jim Crow.

"In the books about the history of photography in Arkansas, the Prellers were never mentioned."

Greer Lile, Photographer/Historian

Preserving the Legacy

The restoration of *The Preller Collection* began 60 years ago when Hugo and Gayne's granddaughter, Gayne Preller Schmidt, began to save their work. Although the collection was dispersed and exposed to the elements over the years, Ms. Schmidt is alone to be thanked for safeguarding the collection all these years.

Yet sometimes it takes an outsider to recognize the wider appeal of local art and documentation, and that's where *The Preller Collection* lived up to its association with the White River. I had paddled 400 miles of the river to reach Augusta to find out about the Preller photographs. When I walked into Gayne's Garments and Goodies in Augusta, and Ms. Schmidt allowed me to see the Preller's glass negatives and prints, the rest was history.

I soon realized we were preserving the work of *two* significant artists and had embarked on the restoration of one of the most important photographic archives to emerge from the Mississippi Delta. Gayne and I forged a partnership to bring the Preller's work to public attention.

We formed an advisory group and, in partnership with the Old Independence Regional Museum in Batesville, secured a grant from the Arkansas Humanities Council to exhibit the collection. Early on, the late photographer-historian, Greer Lile, became a project supporter and granted use of his model of the Preller's floating gallery. He steered us toward a deeper appreciation of Hugo and Gayne's historical significance and artistic legacy.

Playing Gayne Preller in a film for the exhibition, painter-actress Melissa Garrison evaluates glass plates and prints by candlelight aboard the floating gallery.

The Preller's Enduring Spirit

Hugo and Gayne displayed an intrepid pioneering spirit from the time they met until their last days. The life they built together was idyllic—maybe even utopian—a remarkable blending of priorities: family, religion, community and entrepreneurship. They epitomize wholesome, small-town American values, and they captured this with their cameras. In looking at their pictures today, one harks back to their "old-fashioned" era and wonder what it was like to live in a small town, run a local independent business, and remain in one place for half a century. Mrs. Preller tends to the children, stokes a wood cooking stove, orders supplies, meets clients, and markets her pictures. Hugo tinkers at his jeweler's desk, paints on mussel shells, writes his treatise on Genesis, swims in the river, and squirrel hunts with their boys. The children are raised successfully. Neither spouse runs off with another love interest. Clients flock to the Preller Variety Shop, and it prospers financially, while the Prellers remain humble and don't put on airs. Every loving couple should be so lucky to find a soul mate as they did, and turn their lives into an indelible and triumphant tale.

The granddaughter (Gayne Preller Schmidt) and great granddaughters (Ambr, Patti, and Anne) of Hugo and Gayne Preller in 2014.

    I contemplated what might be the underlying theme of their lives, since their story resonates with so many people 100 years later. I decided to put this question to the hundreds of people who were following the Preller exhibition online. I asked them: *What did they admire about the Prellers?*

    Here are some of their responses—

"They're fearless."
"They persevere."
"They're resourceful."
"They work together."
"They're inclusive."
"They aren't affected by fads."
"They remain close to nature."
"They were creative artists but lived by traditional values."

As dusty boxes and crinkled letters revealed the family's story, I recognized that the Preller saga is one of the great stories in the history of American photography. Gayne Laura Avey, only sixteen when they married, seems to follow a path in life laid with Appian stone, straight and without veering in its advance. Storms and tragedy don't alter her aims and duties, which are fused as naturally as cloud and sky. She had chutzpah and was a born adventurer who pioneered in new territory, far away from the security and comforts of her upbringing. By age 19, she is already pugnaciously pursuing an avocation she is intent upon turning into a profession, and this in an era when women rarely envisioned independently supporting themselves. Though her voice is not recorded in memoir, what is seen in family photos is a seasoned woman able to live graciously in the midst of

"A Man and His Hounds," a posed environmental portrait by Hugo Arthur Preller, circa 1920.

hardship. Yet she could not have accomplished what she did without Hugo.

Hugo Arthur Preller was as troubled as any spiritual seeker, a frontier man in search of the sublime. He fits the hero mold of Odysseus, forced onto a dangerous and lonely journey when young, never to see his parents or homeland again. Fearless in adapting to a new land and language, inquisitive and resourceful, he proves to be a man of many talents. With only an incomplete high school education, he independently hones his innate artistic skills. Yet his talents for painting and drawing would remain largely unrealized because he was committed to supporting his family. Spending most of his working hours hunched over his Lilliputian watch and jewelry work, Hugo was a tireless provider. He earned enough for the family to enjoy luxuries that many people did not. But during the Depression, the bank in Augusta was feared to "bust" and he was compensated for his lost deposits with 80 acres of land. This was a rough patch for the Prellers and Gayne's photography business was crucial in making ends meet. After that, Hugo kept his cash in the proverbial mattress at home.

"Mrs. Dillon," portrait by Gayne Preller, circa 1925.

Mr. Preller was also profoundly principled. Never did he flaunt the money he and Gayne earned, or the lifestyle that they achieved. Yet all of this is secondary to his fearless search for spiritual clarity made resolute by an undying need to explain the divine vision he experienced as a child, which we will address in a moment.

The Preller's Photographic Legacy

The Preller Collection depicts the diversity of rural society while also telling the epic story of the Preller family. Moreover, it includes an unprecedented subset of images of African Americans living in the vicinity at the time. Even so, one must ask whether the pictures rise to the level of art. In the case of Gayne Preller's portraiture -- which comprises the great majority of Preller pictures -- one might ask if her pictures are important beyond their historical significance, like those by other female photographers of the era, such as Dorothea Lange, Laura Gilpin, and Imogen Cunningham.

"Mother and Daughter," portrait by Gayne Preller, circa 1915.

At the outset, it seems unfair to measure Gayne's artistic legacy in light of the limiting factors on her life. She was not born into high society; she never attended college. She married very young and gave birth to eight children, four of whom she cared for to adulthood. Moreover, she was culturally isolated from major centers of art and photography, starting her career while living on the Mississippi River and refining it in a small community in the Arkansas Delta. For most, these obstacles would have steered one into a more pedestrian profession. Yet Gayne worked as a photographer continuously, on land and on water, for over 50 years, producing thousands of images which her community paid her to produce. The fact she accomplished this in the Delta, and did so during years that spanned the Great Depression, is central to her legacy and that of the Prellers.

The Purpose of Portraiture

Any conclusions should be prefaced by defining what a photographic portrait is, and how to judge whether one is true art. A portrait is not an impromptu snapshot, but is marked by the subjects knowledge that he or she is being pictured. Hence, a portrait is often said to reveal as much about the portraitist's feeling about the subject, as what the subject feels about himself or herself.

There are types of portraits. An "environmental" portrait is one made in the field, outside the controlled confines of a studio. A publisher who needs a picture to illustrate a body of text often commissions such a portrait. Before photography had proliferated, studio portraits were often commissioned as well, with the photographer hired to document interesting individuals and groups for use in magazines or books. By the turn of the 20th century, however, portraits were commissioned by the subject himself/herself, motivated by personal incentives. American portraiture during Gayne's career was nearly always solicited and used by the sitters themselves. The best portraitist would be someone sensitive to the sitter's motives, and who could selflessly gratify that intent in a final print. Thus the best portrait depicts the projection of a person's desired self-image, not merely what the photographer perceives as special about the person. Revealing portraits also show us what the subject feels about himself or herself. An adept photographer understands how to stay out of the way of this transaction. Gayne was clearly masterful in this; her guiding hand is nearly invisible throughout her work.

Embedded Meaning. There is artificiality in studio portraiture—

"Mr. Crumb," photographed onboard the Preller's floating studio, circa 1900. This portrait validates this man's rising status by featuring his tailored clothes and formal demeanor.

room for acting, conjuring, fakery, yet also the greatest potential for communicating the subject's identity to the viewer. Traditional American portraiture placed people in artificial sets that reinforced notions of identity and social standing. The portrait allowed people to represent their relationship to others and their community. In the darkroom, a portrait was "fixed," and indeed, it provided a new way by which an individual, family or group could "get a fix" on who they were and where they fit in. A photographic portrait is more than a memento. It is a prized family possession, a display of social function, continuity and inclusion. Portraits stop time and cement one's sense of identity. They portray our aspirations and our status in the hierarchy of our community. A cabinet card worked to clarify one's status in relationship to peers and family. It reinforced traditions and group experience. Embodied in a portrait are notions about felt status, personality, wealth, talent, appearance, all of which a paying customer could present to a new visual marketplace. As fast as digital images have spread during our lives, cabinet cards, postcard photographs and stereoscopic images became widely known and popular due to the human needs and desires they served, as well as their technical novelty.

The eloquence of Gayne's vision in an unflinching portrait of rural reality. The family might be poor, but what we see is family pride and cohesion intact. The photographer captures the family as it perceives itself, as human beings rather than symbols.

In the rural South, getting a studio portrait done was nothing less than an act of joining the national transformation from rural parochialism to participation in the modern mainstream. A Southern rural portrait represents the reconciliation of an antebellum past and a modern future. The poor tenant-farming family enters the studio to participate in the new social ritual called photographic portraiture. Gayne's resulting print "fixes" the family betwixt the plantation past and the oncoming future, symbolized on the street outside her studio by the traffic jam of horse-drawn buggies and new Fords. Having a portrait made was empowering; part of its unstated purpose was to foster a myth of high status, a lifestyle of leisure and education—not, I might add, unlike the way photographs are used today on social networks. The props and background conspired to provide the artifice for the personal or group myth to be cast. They are often handy symbols of upward mobility and social power. Books represent education, not always accessible to the rural poor. Musical instruments represent a luxury of leisure time in an era when working hours and wages were miserable. Hugo's backdrops placed people amidst the gardens and architecture of classical Europe, where the meditative arts could be pursued *ad infinitum*. The table, vase and wicker chair lend an aura of domestic calm, even bourgeois refinement.

"Proud Mary," portrait by Gayne Preller, circa 1910.

    The rural citizen is captured in a modern guise; we do not see the implements of his or her trade—the worn tools, animal tack, and farm supplies—which might remind us of the relentless manual labor that most of these people performed. The Prellers did not, however, provide sitters with clothing that might have completed the "fixing" of the intended myth. Clothing bespeaks the actual situation endured by rural people in Woodruff County. Even their Saturday "best" is often ill-fitting, homespun, and tattered beyond mending (see photo on page 111).

The Vitality of Preller Portraits

To fairly assess the merit of the Preller's portrait work, a clear statement of what constitutes an important portrait is needed. Chris Johns, in *National Geographic's* compendium, *In Focus: National Geographic Greatest Portraits*, provides a usable litmus test:

> *"In each portrait there is an individual, with a life and a story to tell. And maybe, just maybe, if the connection between the photographer and subject is trusting enough, and the photographer's skills and sensitivity are high enough, the portrait will reveal the spirit and essence of the individual."*

Beginning with the work the Prellers did while onboard the floating gallery, which likely featured Hugo behind the camera, one can say that the work was formal and more about the pose and atmosphere than revelation of character. Gayne's work, begun in earnest in her Augusta studio, quickly became more intimate; clearly, a compulsion to record human idiosyncrasy suffused her solo work. Unlike the typical portrait studio hack of the era, Gayne was more than a recorder of people's countenances. She closed the distance between camera and subject, looking for an explosion of expression that revealed personality. While Hugo was most keen to photograph (and paint) human events and accomplishments, Gayne was interested in memorializing the affection between mother and child, or between two sisters, or the apparent stoicism of a

"Man with a Pistol," circa 1915.
Photograph by Gayne Preller.

farmstead family. I think her customers got excited about this; it was her value-added.

Subjects are always engaged with Gayne, visually and personally. Always there is affinity and interaction. No person is objectified or abstracted. Look at "The Student," (on page 96). Gayne does not demean her subject by portraying him as underprivileged by the social system. Her intention is to reveal the dream of education and confident search for opportunity. She probes for a rendering of the sitter's self-image, and this also marks her as more modern than the typical studio photographer of the time.

Gayne's style was marked by unabashed sensitivity to her subjects. Her work was devoid of the self-consciousness of modernism, or a political point-of-view, such as in Depression photography in California, in which men and women are often rendered to represent the larger aspirations of a constituency. Gayne's work never attempts to forge such representations. The viewer does not experience Gayne's pictures as "Depression" photography or even "Delta" photography. Her mission is never humanitarian; she only attempts to capture people putting forth their most attractive aspects. In her work we have a sort of community scrapbook that stands on its own merit. One surely senses the Depression years and see it clearly in the gaunt faces of sharecroppers, but history is revealed inadvertently, without artist intent.

An advertisement, circa 1920, that the Prellers ran in the local newspaper.

If a meal line formed in Augusta, would Gayne have photographed it? Not likely. Her work is never critical of the

In one of the finest Preller portraits, Gayne has applied natural lighting from a window to the left, and placed her subjects in front of a neutral backdrop. The geometry of the arms and hands form a square frame that ties the portrait together both compositionally and emotionally.

socio-economic scene in America, or the South. Should we call this "naïve portraiture," given the hard times and injustices that marked her times? If Gayne had been pursuing art photography, it could be seen as blinkered, but she was a commercial portraitist. Gayne was not a stylist or enforcer of an artiste-imposed perspective. She is interested solely in depicting her subject's best side and she is selfless in this pursuit. This is the reason her pictures can be trusted. She's without agenda—we see people projecting their innermost notions of themselves.

Consider "Man With a Pistol," on page 114. A young man camps it up with a real pistol, likely from Hugo's wall in his gun repair shop. The influence of Hollywood is here, a romanticizing of criminality. Clearly, the man's self-image allows for buffoonery and gunplay, hardly an image he *should* present to the world, especially in a photograph. But it *is* the image he feels strongly about, and Gayne accommodates. The result is refreshing authenticity. Another approach might have been contrived and unrevealing. She de-caricaturizes the visual record of her era by *not* engaging in forced artistic interpretation.

Gayne's darkroom technique was non-invasive as well. Like most vintage photographs, her images are rarely cropped. Most are contact prints, not enlargements at all, but a perfect transfer from the original. This heightens their authenticity also. We see the entire view without interpretation.

Gayne Preller was pragmatic in her photographic practice. Her studio was a business, her portrait-making a service. For her, engaging in "art photography" would have been unprofitable; and engaging in politics would have been risky. Like nearby photographer Mike Meyer (Disfarmer), she remained a small-town studio portraitist to the end. The plight of the masses was of little interest to either of these yeoman portraitists, not because they were hard-hearted, but because of the isolation and insularity of the region where they worked.

Comparing Gayne To Disfarmer. Gayne Preller and Mike Meyer (Disfarmer) both worked diligently and reclusively for four

Gayne's portrait of two brothers was made in the late 1930s after she stopped using Hugo's painted backdrops. The portrait is similar to a Disfarmer portrait in the symmetry of its composition and use of a featureless background.

decades in their Arkansas studios. Meyer was born in 1884, nine years after Gayne and twenty years after Hugo. He grew up in the Arkansas Delta, in Stuttgart, the son of a rice farmer who, like Hugo, was of German descent. Sadly, his father died when he was 14 and his mother moved the family to Heber Springs. The Meyer's no longer pursued farming like most people in Cleburne County, and Mike needed to find a profession. He entered the unlikely business of studio portraiture. Unlikely, because he was introverted and cerebral—not a typical candidate for a people business like portraiture. But like Hugo, he was technically skillful. It didn't take him long to master a view camera, process plates, and even improvise an effective electric lighting system.

   Although he also shot landscapes, Meyer has become famous for his oeuvre of portraits of Heber Springs residents, mostly made in the 1930s and 40s. I personally cannot imagine his clients cherishing many of the portraits he made of them. Meyer placed his sitters against monotone backdrops and made full-body shots with the objectivity of a police photographer. My wife detests his pictures, thinking they are disrespectful, if not downright mean. To my 17-year-old son, they are just dull. But to modernist eyes – including my own – Meyer's work is riveting. He may have failed some of his clients who sought cuddly family mementos, but his portraits penetrate to the core of the human condition. While Gayne's work ennobles individuals, Meyer's images render them anonymous. While Meyer's work is revealing of the hard realities of southern rural society, Gayne's work celebrates individual strength and resiliency. Gayne is associative, portraying human interaction, while Meyer is dissociative, depicting the existential exigencies of aloneness, loss, failed ambition and irrelevance. His collection contains no people of color (few, if any, Africans Americans lived in Heber Springs at the time) and few pictures that connect his subjects to the pastimes of their lives.

   But like Gayne, Meyer's style never altered direction with shifting aesthetic winds blowing from the coasts. He never sustained contact with contemporaries like Lange, Bourke-White, and Frank Capa, or submitted work for national publication. Moreover, neither Gayne nor Meyer were interested in the politics of social reform. Neither considered themselves artists, nor does their work embody an artist's subjectivity. Ironically, both created work that was supremely about people, the difference being that Meyer wasn't particularly fond of them while Gayne genuinely was. Like Gayne, Meyer stayed in the decidedly unglamorous portrait business because it was steady work—it paid the bills and put food on the table.

But Mike Meyer out-distanced Gayne technically. He was a skilled camera operator and he used a large reflector and a bare-bulb flash to freeze his subject's expressions, as well as cast a hard relief of shadows over clothing and facial lines that lent an exacting sharpness to his prints. Gayne's images are soft by comparison, sharp in one plane but out of focus in another. The effect in her work is pictorial and would be considered amateurish by many collectors today. When Hugo's painterly backdrops wore out and lost fashion, Gayne installed stale-looking white drapery. Meanwhile Meyer fashioned canvas-covered boards on wheels connected with painted vertical stripes. The effect is Japanesque and pleasing to the modern eye; his pictures don't look antique. While Meyer is compared to Weegee and Diane Arbus, Mrs. Preller can only be compared to earlier era photographers.

Was Gayne a Feminist?

Absolutely she was, if one takes 'feminist' to mean the dictionary definition as a person who advocates for equal rights for women. Yet she was not a rights activist; she was a feminist by example. She exuded an enlightened and positive outlook and hoped to inspire other women with her attitude. She encouraged her granddaughter first in piano playing and then in photography, not as much because the arts were important to her, but because the pursuit and refinement of a woman's talent toward making a livelihood was essential in her mind. By developing her potential while young, Mrs. Preller had brought

"Bonnie," circa 1915. A portrait by Gayne Preller that displays sensitivity to the incentives of her subject and hints at intimate photography in the future.

home the bacon. Her art sustained her family and provided her an independent lifestyle that few women of her time and place achieved. By example, she advocated female empowerment through applied education and mastery of skills.

For Mrs. Preller, women were equal members of society, deserving equal treatment and a chance to achieve fulfilling lives. She seems to understand and rally for the desires and dreams of the women she photographed. She depicts many types of women, without judgment or prejudice, from aspiring models and flappers to temperance dames and actresses from the local Shakespeare club. And I believe she influenced the thinking of many of the women whom she photographed. Doubtless, Gayne's early work displays a flair for the delicate debutante perfectly lighted, lily white, with a corsage in her styled hair. But contrast this approach to the picture of "Bonnie," (above). The viewer is not being proffered a 'type' of woman here, but an individual who elicits questions about her personality. She is portrayed as confident, at ease with her body, sensual. Is the photo risqué? Yes! It would have been considered downright improper by the deacons of morality in Augusta. Even to us, it hints at intimate portraiture or boudoir photography. Once again, Gayne has chosen to go where the customer wants to take the picture.

Gayne Preller's work is about connection. She portrays the warm embrace between people, and between herself and her subjects. In her pictures one feels the bond she formed with her village.

A Timeless Portrait of a Delta Community

Like William Faulkner's mythical Yoknapatawpha County, the Preller's "physiognomy of a community" reconnects us to a distant and different past. Produced in a single cultural region of the country, much of the collection's value is due to its narrow focus and the tumultuous period during which the photographs were made.

"The Courting," by Hugo or Gayne Preller,
or both working together. Circa, 1915.

Both Hugo and Gayne painted and made photos as if they knew how fast their world was changing and how quickly it would vanish. Perhaps because they descended the rivers themselves, they were aware of the momentous social and ecological changes taking place all around them. Their lives unfold between a traditional and a transformed Delta. Their work looks backward and ahead, feeling both vintage and modern simultaneously. Their collection is an act of time travel, a vast photographic narrative detailing the story of a community's emergence.

Gayne Preller possessed the perfect sensibility to make this connection with everyday people and bring out the spirit of their personalities in photographs. As a portrait artist, Mrs. Preller passes Chris Johns' litmus test in all of his criteria, save one. And that is in the area of "skills." Gayne's technique remained only half-realized, due purely to her extreme isolation from photographic advances and aesthetic breakthroughs that were taking place on the coasts of America and in Europe. There is a roughshod quality to her studio work, and a peculiar absence of incremental innovation that one would expect from a serious photographer working consistently over a span of fifty years. Yet, while this deficiency all but excludes Mrs. Preller from an elite group including Käsebrier, Lange, Cunningham and Gilpin, it cannot negate the authentic and singular body of work she produced, especially in light of its social and historical value.

Hence, it is fair to say that both of the Prellers were significant regional photographers, and that *The Preller Collection* as a whole is one of the most important archives to emerge from turn-of-the-century southern America. This, in tandem with the mythic qualities of the Preller family story, imbues the collection with enduring charm and value.

Preparation for exhibiting *The Preller Collection* began with a design schematic for the Horace C. Cabe Gallery at the Historic Arkansas Museum in Little Rock. The exhibit is divided into six narrative sections, based on the chapters of this book, and features a model of the Preller's floating studio fashioned by photographer-historian Greer Lile.

A page from Hugo Preller's 725-page manuscript, safeguarded for 65 years by his granddaughter, Gayne Preller Schmidt.

Epilogue

The Meaning of Hugo Preller's Vision

I began this tale in search of Hugo Arthur Preller. During the last days of archiving the collection, I finally found him when I learned of his 725-page handwritten manuscript that sits in a cardboard box next to his Bible in his granddaughter's conservatory in Augusta. She has protected it more guardedly than any other Preller artifact in her possession. The delicate century-old pages contain Mr. Preller's spiritual declarations laid down at the end of a lifetime of seeking, preaching, and turning the other cheek toward his church elders.

Some years ago, Ms. Schmidt took on the yeoman task of transcribing the manuscript and keyed in several thousand of its quilled words. Throughout the treatise, one senses the urgency that drove Mr. Preller in quest of explanations concerning the truth about man's genesis, the ultimate intentions of God, and perhaps more than anything, the agonizing riddle of the childhood hallucination that never gave him peace. Thankfully, after 75 years, his vision finally revealed its mystery and he was able to set down its interpretation before his passing.

"I heard a woman scream," he begins, recounting the seconds after a ball of fire flew across a lake, passed him with a hissing sound, and streaked through an adjacent farm. "And I will always believe that she was frightened by the sight of this same ball of fire rushing by her and over the earth." This was proof that the little boy walking home on a winter's morning had not imagined the experience.

Though he was a youngster when it happened, Hugo describes how its indelible memory grew in significance during his life, especially after he learned of similar phenomena occurring in Scripture. In Joel (II.28), he found the prophecy stating that when the end time nears, "Young men shall see visions." Suspecting a hidden meaning to his vision, he visited with church leaders, psychologists, philosophers, and even New Thought teachers in search of answers. But no one, he grumbled, offered a hint of an explanation. Moreover, not one was even "inclined to enter into any discussion" about the significance of the apparition. He concluded that the true interpretation of such a dream can only come from God, and that such "rare, supernatural" visions are "beyond the wisdom of man" to understand at all. He further reasoned that since man is incapable of interpreting God's word in Scripture, true religious illumination would, therefore, need to be sent to earth in the form of dreams manifested in the minds of "servants and handmaidens of the Lord."

Thinking that he must be one of these chosen few, Hugo came to believe that his earliest desire "to become a laborer in the vineyard of the Lord" was a fulfillment of his youthful vision. He etched its inescapable meaning with a frantic quill: "A child returning to the Father's house from a journey." This, he construed, signified "the return to God the Father of the Adamic man." The dense clouds and the earth covered with a mantle of ice became emblematic of "the true light of heaven hidden in a cloud of unbelief." (Hugo was forever ranting about the comatose state of spiritual life in modern society.) A child skips along, "indifferent to [the] gathering darkness and deathlike stillness." To the adult Hugo, the scene translated as "the indifference of the world to the teachings of Christ," and underscored "the spirit of frivolity and sport manifested today the world over."

And then a ball of fire rose from the frozen waters. For him, this was "God's love for a dying, sin-cursed world," a final wakeup call and warning before the promised "wrath to come." His childhood vision had morphed into a personalized *Revelation of St. John the Divine*.

> *And, behold, I come quickly.... I am the Alpha*
> *and the Omega, the beginning and the end....*
> *And let him who is athirst come.*

Hugo imagined that even atheists would "take of the water of life

In an oil painting by Hugo Preller circa 1903, and now in need of restoration, the artist displays his documentary prowess. We witness a levee building operation, probably along the Missisiippi River, replete with mule teams, corrals, and crew encampment. Preller family member, Melanie Alumbaugh, donated the piece to the Jacksonport State Park several years ago. *Courtesy of Jacksonport State Park.*

freely" and directly from him, since, "by a higher authority, the spirit has revealed unto [me] the true interpretation of [my] vision in childhood days."

But thirsty souls did not come to hear Mr. Preller's "true interpretation of the Word of God." His devotion had become obsessive, his spiritualism rigid, and his humanity bitter. Immersed for endless hours in his silent work, he withdrew from neighbors, friends, and even his family. In his manuscript, he challenged his audience to "judge for themselves, for [my] words and work will bear their own credentials." But his devoutness was too strict, cerebral, and without connection to others, even to his wife.

Hugo and Gayne had lived separate lives for years now. Though their bond was never broken, one can guess that Gayne was less than satisfied at this time. She cared for Hugo during the two years he remained bedridden, feeding and bathing him. When the end came, a funeral was held that was not well attended. At its conclusion, Mrs. Preller turned to her granddaughter and half-joked: "Honey, if I live to be a hundred, don't let me marry another one like Hugo." Although uttered without malice, the feeling was clear. She had lived for too long without the companionship, affection, and warmth that she and Hugo once shared.

Yet we shall not end our story on an unpleasant chord. Not long after Hugo's passing, one of his sons and a cousin were helping Mrs. Preller clean up Hugo's shop, gathering his tools and boxing up his guns and Swiss-made watch parts. Beneath the jeweler's desk at which he spent so much of his later years, they discovered his green tool chest. They emptied the toolbox and found at its base a false bottom with a finger hole. They lifted it out and were amazed to find "more cash than they had ever seen in one place," recalls Ms. Schmidt. Even in death, Hugo remained a devoted provider for his family and his wife.

Though silver and gold be beneath thy feet;
and treasures be at thy command:
What can they profit while they
remain hidden 'neath gravel and sand?

Even so treasures of wisdom and truth;
how can the world thereby gain?
How can the hungry soul feed upon things
which it is refused to obtain?

Go! Write the vision, and make it plain;
That he that readeth may run,
with patience the voice set before every one;
and by which life's crown may be won.

This is the Lord's, the Creator's command;
Let every one heed it and strive;
to follow the narrow path to the straight gate,
that offers an entrance to life.

Hugo Arthur Preller, 1929

SUGGESTED READING
(Alphabetized by title)

A Concise History of Photography, by Helmut Gernsheim. New York: Gosset & Dunlap: 1965. An accessible introduction to the major milestones and personalities.

Arkansas: A Narrative History. Jeannie M. Whayne et al. The University of Arkansas Press: Fayetteville, 2013. An overview of the key events with engaging interpretation.

Dialogue with Photography, by Paul Hill, and Thomas Cooper. Dewi Lewis: England: 1979. A good share of the world's important photographers interviewed, including Preller contemporaries.

White River Memoirs: the Spoken History of a Liquid Legend, by Chris Engholm. Road of Awe art & media: 2014. An oral history that includes an interview with Gayne Preller Schmidt speaking about Hugo and Gayne Preller.

In Focus: National Geographic Greatest Portraits. National Geographic Society: 2004. *(The quote from Chris Johns on page 113 of this book appears on page 25 in this title.)*

Life On the Mississippi, by Mark Twain. A romp on the Big Muddy before the Civil war, with descriptions of steamboat operations and ports the Prellers visited forty years later.

Rivers and Roads and Points In Between. Woodruff County Historical Society: Augusta, Arkansas. All years and issues enlighten and entertain those interested in Delta community history.

Steamboats and Ferries on the White River: A Heritage Revisited. Duane Huddleston, et al. UCA Press: Conway, Arkansas, 1995. A preeminent history, including mention and a photo of the Preller's floating studio.

Two Centuries of Methodism in Arkansas, by Nancy Britton. August House Publishers: Little Rock. 2000. A rare account that helps fill in the undocumented period when Hugo Preller was a Methodist preacher.

(The quote appearing on page 33 of this book is from page 48 of Britton's book.)

The Arkansas Delta: A Landscape of Change. The Delta Cultural Center: Helena, Arkansas: 1990. This catalog to an exhibition provides a well-illustrated overview of the region's history, ecology, society, and culture.

The Strange Career of Jim Crow. C. Vann Woodward. Oxford University Press. 1955. An enduring assessment of racial segregation in America prior to the civil rights movement.

Wild Sports in the Far West. Frederick Gerstaecker. Crosby, Nichols, and Company: Boston, 1859. Another German visitor finds a muse in the Arkansas Delta fifty years before Hugo Preller.

Women's America: Refocusing the Past, by Linda K. Kerber and Jane Sherron De Hart. Oxford University Press: New York, 1982. A well-documented American history reader from a women's studies perspective.

Official Preller Website

www.facebook.com/HugoArthurPreller

Guests at the opening reception for *Hugo and Gayne Prellers' House of Light*, at Old Independence Regional Museum in Batesville, Arkansas on April 14, 2014.

INDEX

A

African Americans, 22, 76, 85, 86, 88, 89, 88, 91, 93, 95, 97, 98, 99, 101, 108, 117
Allyn Lord, 5
America (USA), 19, 21, 22, 26, 29, 75, 85, 97, 101, 117, 124, 134
anti-German sentiment, 99-100
Arkansas Advocate (1929), 76
Arkansas Delta, 3, 9, 26, 36, 43, 44, 49, 53, 55, 56, 60, 61, 68, 85, 88, 89, 97, 101, 108, 109, 115, 119, 122, 124, 132, 133
Arkansas Historic Museum, 21
Arkansas Humanities Council, 5
Augusta, Arkansas, 9, 29, 44, 51, 52, 55, 56, 68, 69, 70, 71, 76, 80, 86, 88, 89, 99, 101, 107, 113, 115, 122, 132
Avey, Issac, 54

B

backdrop, photographic, 42, 55, 63, 72, 112, 119
Bentonville, Arkansas, 1, 11
Biblical philosophy, 98
book (design) notes, 137

C

cabinet card (photo), 27, 55, 76, 111
California, 115
carte de visité photographs, 76
Civil War (U.S.), 22, 23, 36, 78, 96, 97
Cleburne County, AR, 119
Columbus, Kentucky, 22, 23, 24, 29, 34, 35, 41, 42, 53
contact printing, 72, 73
cotton, 88, 97

Crocketts Bluff, AR., 44
Cunningham, Imogen, 61, 63, 89, 109

D

darkroom, 72, 75, 111, 117
DeBaun, Robert, 101
Depression, Great, 74, 107, 109, 115
DeValls Bluff, AR., 44
digital images, 112

E

Engholm, Chris, 1, 3, 7, 9, 132
enlarger, photographic, 75
Evans, Walker, 61

F

Faulkner, William, 123
feminism, 121
film camera, 73
floating studio, 3, 5, 13, 26, 27, 28, 42, 55, 56, 69, 80, 99, 131
Friedrich Preller the Elder, 19
Friedrich Preller the Younger, 19, 21

G

Garrison, Melissa, 5, 11
Germany, 11, 21, 29, 33, 34, 36, 44, 100
Gerstaeker, Friedrich, 34, 36
Gilpin, Laura, 61, 108
glass negatives, 13, 52, 63, 73, 75

H

Heber Springs, AR, 119
Historic Arkansas Museum, 5
Hitler, Adolf, 100

Homer's Odyssey, 20
House of Doors studio, 66, 78, 81, 91, 93, 102
House of Doors, The, 13, 29, 51, 56, 66, 70, 80, 89
House of Light, A, exhibition, 1, 3, 5, 14, 31, 51, 66, 106, 134
houseboat (the Preller's), 25, 28, 41, 42, 54, 55, 69
humurous photographs, 76

J

Jesus Christ, 33, 101
jeweler's desk, (Hugo Preller's) 80, 105
Jim Crow, 85, 86, 90, 91, 93, 101, 133
Johns, Chris, 113, 132

K

Käsebrier, Gertrude, 124
Kentucky Trail, 22, 33, 53
Kodak, 73

L

Lange, Dorothea, 13, 61, 107
letters, 13, 37, 38, 40, 41, 46
levee building (painting), 129
Lile, Greer, 5, 68, 70, 80, 81

M

media, photographic, 74
Memphis, Tennessee, 23, 25, 29, 34, 35, 36, 37, 38, 39, 41, 61, 86, 95, 97, 98, 99
Methodist Church, 22, 33, 101, 132
Meyer, Mike (Disfarmer), 64, 117, 119
Mississippi River, 3, 22, 23, 24, 29, 33, 34, 35, 44, 51, 55, 108, 132
Modotti, Tina, 13

N

Naturalization papers (Hugo Preller), 21
New South, the, 22, 25, 43

O

Old Independence Regional Museum, 5

P

photography, 13, 24, 26, 29, 39, 42, 43, 51, 52, 53, 54, 55, 57, 60, 61, 71, 73, 80, 89, 91, 94, 106-121
pictorialism, 57, 59
portrait studio, 3, 29, 60, 114
portraits, 3, 26, 29, 55, 59, 60, 71, 76, 96, 109-120, 125
portraiture, 26, 55, 56, 63, 109, 112, 113, 118, 120, 123
post card photographs, 76
Preller children, 78
Preller TV (repair shop), 9
Preller Variety Shop, 56, 70, 78, 79, 80, 91, 106
Preller, Gayne Laura, 1, 3, 9, 11, 13, 19, 23, 24, 25, 27, 28, 29, 33, 35, 37, 38, 41, 42, 51, 52, 53, 54, 55, 56, 57, 58, 59, 60, 61, 63, 64, 68, 70, 71, 72, 73, 75, 79, 80, 81, 85-95, 98, 100, 101, 102, 106, 106-124
Preller, Hugo Arthur, 1, 3, 9, 11, 13, 19, 22, 25, 27, 29, 33, 34, 35, 37, 38, 39, 40, 42, 43, 44, 46, 51, 52, 53, 54, 55, 56, 59, 61, 67, 68, 69, 71, 74, 78, 79, 80, 95, 97, 98, 99, 103, 105, 111, 115, 117, 118, 124, 128-132
Preller, Max, 78, 79, 80
Preller, Victor II, 25, 38, 41, 42, 68

R

Reconstruction, 22, 85, 97
Red Cross, 93
river justice, 97

S

Schmidt, Gayne Preller, 1, 9, 11, 21, 51, 69, 72, 79, 80, 83, 84, 87
Schroeter, H.O., 27
Scripture, Biblical, 79, 99
sharecroppers, 56, 63, 88, 93, 115
slavery, 99
snapshots, 60, 109
SS Spain, 21
St. Louis, Missouri, 23, 25, 26, 29, 34, 37, 40, 41, 42, 44, 61
Stieglitz, Alfred, 61
studio portraiture, 111, 119

T

tenant farming, 83, 87, 88, 90, 111
The Preller Collection, 3, 9, 76, 107, 123
Twain, Mark, 23, 35, 44, 132

U

University of Central Arkansas, 5

V

vision, religious, (Hugo Preller's) 46, 127-129
Voss, Carey, 21

W

Websites (about the Prellers), 133
Weston, Edward, 13
White River, (Arkansas), 9, 11, 29, 36, 37, 38, 44, 51, 68, 100, 132
Woodruff County, AR, 56, 76, 78, 99, 113, 132
WPA photography, 61, 93

Book notes

The text of this book was set in Century Gothic, a font based on an earlier style called 20th Century designed by Sol Hess between 1936 and 1947. Made suitable for digital printers of today, Century Gothic is nonetheless a tribute to the modernist geometric sans serif faces of the 1920s and 30s.

The Preller's art and photographic prints were reproduced using Nikon digital cameras and macro lenses under natural light. Adobe Photoshop was used to remove blemishes and tone the images to appear as they would have when they emerged from the Preller's darkroom. Some glass plates were photographed using film and printed on traditional silver gelatin photographic paper. The book was designed by Chris Engholm in Microsoft Word.

Published by roadofawe art & media in Bentonville, Arkansas.

To contact the author, report errors, or permissions, email: **roadofawe@gmail.com**.

"This for That," a clever sketch by Hugo Preller in which cherubs trade 'new ideas' for a bag of money, and commercial transporation eclipses the traditional pastoral mode of life that the artist loved. Date unknown.

Made in the USA
San Bernardino, CA
31 January 2017